The Big Book of
Thematic Plays

25 Exciting, Easy-to-Read Plays with Instant Activities on the Topics You Teach

SCHOLASTIC
PROFESSIONAL BOOKS

New York • Toronto • London • Auckland • Sydney
Mexico City • New Delhi • Hong Kong

Edited by Tracey West
Cover design by Norma Ortiz
Cover art by Anne Kennedy
Interior design by Sydney Wright
Interior art by Paige Billin-Frye

ISBN 0-590-68569-4

Contents

Folk Tales and Myths

School

Community

Science and Health

Introduction

Welcome to *The Big Book of Thematic Plays*! At Scholastic, we know that teachers love using short, fun plays in their classrooms. We also know that it's even better when plays tie in to special days around the year or popular teaching themes. In this book, you'll find 25 plays that do just that. In addition, they have been carefully crafted for use with early elementary students.

Here are just some of the benefits you receive by including plays in your curriculum:

• foster reading skills and build oral literacy

• help children understand plot development through dialogue

• freshen familiar and popular themes

• commemorate important events throughout the school year

• build a sense of community in your classroom

• offer students experience in performing for an audience

• encourage students to be attentive members of an audience

• teach children how to be appreciative of others' efforts

• instill students with a love of the theater, and

• have fun together!

About This Book

This collection of 25 plays is designed to support themes popular with elementary schoolteachers. Some plays offer a fresh spin on classic events and themes (Thanksgiving, the first day of school); other plays were included to boost your curriculum in areas for which you may have a lack of material (Groundhog Day, dental health).

While we have suggested themes for all of the plays in this book, you will find that most plays lend themselves to a variety of themes. The play "A Snowman for Mrs. McKay," for example, could accompany lessons on snow, the seasons, cooperation, the winter holiday season, and community.

Following each play is a teacher's guide designed to both simplify and enhance your efforts to share the plays in class. In each guide you'll find

• Using the Play—suggestions for managing students and staging the play.

• Background Information—a quick collection of facts to introduce or follow up the play experience.

• Book Links—a bibliography of theme-related materials to enhance the excitement generated by the play.

• Extension Activities—cross-curricular ideas to help broaden the play experience.

Ways to Use the Plays

There are lots of ways to share the plays in this book with students. Some require a bit of long-range planning, while others require no preparation at all! Which route you choose—simple or elaborate—is up to you, but here are three basic approaches to consider:

• **Readers Theater:** In this technique, children are assigned parts in the play to read aloud to each other or to an audience. Students often feel best exploring new characters and experimenting with different voices without the burden of memorizing lines or movements. Even children with experience performing in full-scale play productions can benefit from reading a play aloud with classmates.

• **In-Class Skit:** As students become familiar with plays and the play format, they may want to experiment with acting out scripts for each other in class. As kids become more confident and polished, they may want to invite another class over for an informal performance. There is no need to worry about fancy costumes or scenery at this level.

• **Full-Scale Production:** A full-scale production calls for all the theatrical trimmings: costumes, scenery, props, and student actors willing and able to memorize a script and act it out with stage directions for an audience.

Choosing the Right Play

All of the plays in this book were designed to be accessible to your students; however, we made sure to include a number of plays that were appropriate for beginning readers who might have trouble memorizing lines or following complicated stage directions. These plays contain elements like rhyming text and repetition. If you're working with younger students, these plays may be a good choice for you:

Getting to Know You	I Take My Senses Everywhere
The Garden Meal	A Snowman for Mrs. McKay
Mrs. Toodle Bakes a Pie	Peter Penguin's Not Ready Yet
Michael's Cat	A Surprise for the Tooth Fairy

If you're looking for more of a challenge, then try one of these plays:

Dinosaurs With a Difference	The Ocean Olympics
Pecos Bill and Slue-Foot Sue	Great-grandma's Yo-Yo

Whatever you decide, you may want to include your students in the decision-making process: they'll be more enthusiastic about doing a play they handpicked.

Preparing to Perform

When the time comes to ready students for a full-scale play production, there are ways to prepare without the panic.

- **Read-Throughs:** Conduct several informal read-throughs first. The kids will get used to the rhythm of the script and become familiar with the story. When the curtain rises, they will be familiar with the play and where it's headed.

- **Movement Warm-Ups:** Since several of the plays in this book incorporate a lot of movement, certain movement exercises can be very helpful before you begin the play process. For example, if a play contains animal movements, do some animal exercises with the whole class. Explore how different animals would move and sound. Have children "become" the animals in question.

- **Research:** Your students may feel more comfortable with a script if they've researched the topic before doing the play. Tell children that before stepping on the stage, professional actors often conduct long research sessions to acquaint themselves with a character or a time period.

Getting Everyone Involved

Putting on a play is a collaborative effort. Many of the plays in this book are written with enough parts to accommodate any number of students. But what about those plays that do not have enough parts—or enough juicy parts—to go around? One solution is to have several different performance casts. Also, many of the plays feature one or two narrators or storytellers. The lines of the narrator can be divided up among students who don't have speaking parts.

You can also involve interested children in behind-the-scenes action. Students should know that in both professional and amateur theater, there are more jobs than just acting—many talented people work "in the wings" in order to make a production a success.

Children can contribute to the production as:

- Stage Managers
- Prop Masters
- Program Designers
- Costume Designers
- Set Designers
- Ushers

Putting on a Full-Scale Production

Putting on a full-scale production of a play can be both challenging and rewarding. There are many elements that must mesh to ensure your efforts are successful. With a little preplanning and organization, these elements can flow together without a hitch.

- **Casting:** Talk to students about the different roles available. Make sure they understand the responsibility of each.

- **Sets and Props:** Most of the plays in this book are intended to be performed right in your classroom, so the demand for sets and props is minimal. The simple sets and props suggested will enhance the production, but aren't integral to the success of the plays.

- **Promotion:** Have students design posters advertising the performances. Even if your class is putting on a play for only one other class, have students design a poster announcing it to the audience. Students can also design and print programs to hand out to audience members before the performance. These programs can include a synopsis of the play, the names of cast members and production personnel, plus a list of people who deserve special thanks.

- **Parental and Community Involvement:** Play productions are perfect opportunities to develop a connection with the parents and the community. Enlist parents to help in generating costumes, sets, and props. Also collect costumes and props from area businesses. Consider collecting donations at the door and use the proceeds to support a community effort already in progress.

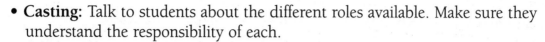

Additional Resources

- *Creative Drama in the Classroom* by Nellie McCaslin (Longman, 1990)
- *Handbook of Educational Drama and Theater* by Robert J. Landy (Greenwood Press, 1982)
- *Plays Around the Year* (Scholastic, 1994)
- *Theater Games for the Classroom—A Teacher's Handbook* by Viola Spolin (Northwestern University Press, 1986)

Home Sweet Home

by Carol Pugliano-Martin

Characters

* Beaver
* Hermit Crab
* Rabbit
* Bear
* Bees
* Bird

Props

* a large box or table for a bear cave
* a child-size box for a beehive
* a pillow for a bird's nest
* a child-size box for a snail shell

Act 1

All of the animals are onstage together.

All Animals: It's time for the animal party!
It's time to dance and sing.
Let's eat lots of tasty food
And say hello to Spring!

Beaver: *[Yawning.]* It's getting dark. I need to get back to my lodge.

Hermit Crab: What's a lodge?

Beaver: A lodge is a beaver home. It is made from sticks and mud.

Rabbit: I must go home to my burrow. That is where my rabbit family lives. It is under the ground.

Bear: I must go home to my cave. It is nice and cozy. My bear cubs are waiting for me there.

Bees: Buzz! We must hurry back to our hive. We bees make honey there.

Hermit Crab: What about you, Bird?

Bird: I am going home to my bird's nest. It is high up in a tree.

Beaver: Are you going home, Hermit Crab?

Hermit Crab: Well, I don't know. I am looking for a new home. I grew too big for my shell. That is where I used to live.

Rabbit: Hey! Maybe we can help you find a new home!

Bear: Sure! Maybe you can live in one of our homes.

Hermit Crab: Well, I guess it's worth a try.

All Animals: Let's go!

Act 2

The animals begin walking in a row. Suddenly, they all stop. They can bump into each other for a slapstick effect.

Bear: Here we are! Here is my cozy cave. Try it out.

Hermit Crab: *[Stands in cave, flailing his arms around.]* Your cave is very nice, Bear. It is cozy for you, but it is way too big for me.

[The animals begin walking again. They stop suddenly and bump into each other again.]

Bees: Buzz! Welcome to our hive! We love it here.

Hermit Crab: *[Squeezes into hive hole, but gets stuck in the honey.]* Your hive is smaller than Bear's cave. But it's too sticky for me.

[The animals begin walking again. One last time, they stop and bump into each other.]

Bird: Climb onto my back, Hermit Crab. I will fly you up to my nest.

[Hermit Crab holds on to Bird's back and they "fly" to the nest. The other animals look up from the ground.]

Bird: Well, what do you think?

Hermit Crab: Your nest is very nice, Bird. But I can't climb this tree all by myself.

Bird: I guess you are right. Let's go.

[Bird and Hermit Crab "fly" out of the nest.]

Hermit Crab: Look! Over there on the beach! It's a snail shell. It looks like it might be just right.

Bird: Let's take a look. *[To the other animals.]* Meet us at the beach!

[Bird and Hermit Crab "fly" to the beach while the other animals walk over.]

Hermit Crab: First, I must see if the shell is empty. *[Peeks in shell.]* Hello! Anybody home? *[Waits.]* I guess not.

Rabbit: Give it a try!

Hermit Crab: OK. *[Hermit Crab crawls into the shell. It's a perfect fit.]* I love it! Thanks for your help!

All Animals: We're so glad you have a home.
It's the greatest thing around.
Now wherever you may roam.
We know where you can be found!

The End

Teacher's Guide

Home Sweet Home

Using the Play

Making animals' homes for the set out of large boxes can be a fun project for the whole class. However, if using boxes is too cumbersome, you may also wish to draw the bear cave, the tree, and the beehive on pieces of chart paper (or larger paper) and hang them on the wall of your performance area.

Background

The main character of this play is a hermit crab. Before introducing the play, ask students if they know what a hermit crab is. Explain that a hermit crab is a kind of crab that lives in a shell cast off by other animals (mollusks, or snails). As the crab gets bigger, it looks for a new, larger shell that will fit. Some students may have hermit crabs as pets, and may be able to relay more information about their behavior.

Besides learning about hermit crabs, children will also learn about other kinds of animal homes when reading this play. Understanding that different animals need different kinds of homes—such as nests, ponds, burrows, warrens, holes in trees, and caves—is an important science concept for young learners. Older learners can expand on this idea by understanding that different habitats, such as oceans, deserts, mountains, forests, and wetlands, provide homes for different varieties of animal life.

Book Links

Animal Homes by Bobbie D. Kalman (Crabtree Publishing, 1994)

Animal Homes by Joyce Pope (Troll Associates, 1993)

Scholastic's The Magic School Bus: Liz Looks for a Home by Tracey West (Scholastic, 1998)

Extending the Play

Animal Home Memory Game

You can put a new spin on the traditional game of Memory by creating Animal Home cards. You'll need to make 6–10 pairs of cards. On one card (index cards work well), draw or paste a picture of an animal. On another card, draw or paste a picture of that animal's home. To play the game, students turn the cards upside down, mix them up, and spread them out on a flat surface. Players take turns overturning 2 cards at a time. If the two cards match— an animal is matched with its home—the player keeps the pair. The game continues until all the cards are matched up, and the player with the most pairs wins.

Here are some sample animal/home pairs you can use:

> frog/pond
> bird/nest
> bear/cave
> squirrel/hollow tree
> ant/anthill
> rabbit/burrow
> bee/hive
> fox/den

Habitat Posters

Divide the class into groups. Assign each group a different habitat—ocean, mountain, forest, desert, wetlands, city, etc. Challenge each group to research the kinds of animals that can be found in that habitat and then create a Habitat Poster on chart paper. Students can draw or paste pictures of the animals on the paper, and can also be encouraged to include a key on the poster that gives the names of the animals and perhaps tells a little something about each one. The Habitat Posters can be displayed in an animal learning center.

Animal Story Graph

If you're using this play to enrich a theme about animals or animal homes, then it's likely that you and your class have shared many animal stories together. Why not make a graph to show which stories children like best?

To make this horizontal bar graph, begin with a large piece of chart paper. Across the top, write "Our Favorite Animal Stories." On index cards, write the names of animal books the class has shared. Paste those cards down the left side of the paper. Have children write their names on index cards and then paste their cards in the horizontal rows next to the name of the book they like the best. To read the graph, look at the length of the horizontal bars. Ask: *Which bar is the longest? Which bar is the shortest? How does this show which books we like best?*

Peter Penguin's Not Ready Yet

by Betsy Franco

Characters

* Narrator

Family 1:
* Mother Penguin 1
* Father Penguin 1
* Betty Penguin

Family 2:
* Mother Penguin 2
* Father Penguin 2
* Sammy Penguin

Family 3:
* Mother Penguin 3
* Father Penguin 3
* Peter Penguin

Props

* rug or sheet to represent an iceberg

Act 1

A penguin rookery in the South Pole. The three baby penguins are rolled up into balls, pretending to be penguin eggs. While the narrator talks, the father and mother penguins take turns sitting on their eggs.

Narrator: The Adélie penguins were at the rookery. A rookery is a group of penguins that live together. The father penguins kept the eggs warm. Then the mother penguins kept the eggs warm. Then it was the father's turn again. Finally, it was time for the eggs to hatch.

Mother Penguin 1: Time to come out, Betty!

Father Penguin 1: Time to come out of your egg!

Betty: *[Popping up.]* Okay, here I come!

Mother Penguin 2: Time to come out, Sammy!

Father Penguin 2: Time to hatch!

Sammy: *[Rubbing eyes, sitting up.]* Okay, here I come!

Mother Penguin 3: Time to come out, Peter!

Father Penguin 3: Time to come out of your egg!

Peter Penguin: *[Staying rolled up in a ball.]* I'm not coming out. I'm not ready yet!

Narrator: Mother Penguin waited. Father Penguin waited. Peter Penguin did not come out. Mother and Father could not wait any longer.

Mother Penguin 3: You must come out today, Peter.

Father Penguin 3: We will count to three.

Mother Penguin 3 & Father Penguin 3: One . . . two . . . three . . .

Peter Penguin: *[Sitting up and smiling.]* I'm out! I'm out! Why didn't I come out sooner?

Act 2

Narrator: Penguins can slide on the ice to get around. They slide on their tummies. It was time for the babies to learn to slide.

Mother Penguin 1: Here's how to slide, Betty. *[Pretends to slide, with arms outstretched.]*

Father Penguin 1: Follow me. *[Pretends to slide.]*

Betty: Okay, here I come! *[Pretends to slide.]*

Mother Penguin 2: Here's how to slide, Sammy. *[Pretends to slide.]*

Father Penguin 2: Watch me. *[Pretends to slide.]*

Sammy: Here I come! *[Pretends to slide.]*

Mother Penguin 3: Time to slide now, Peter.

Father Penguin 3: Follow me, Peter. *[Pretends to slide.]*

Peter Penguin: I'm not going to slide. I'm not ready yet!

Narrator: Mother and Father Penguin waited and waited. But Peter would not slide.

Father Penguin 3: We will count to three, Peter.

Father Penguin 3 & Mother Penguin 3: One . . . two . . . three . . .

Peter Penguin: *[Pretends to slide.]* I'm sliding. I'm sliding. Wheeeee! Why didn't I slide sooner?

Act 3

Narrator: The penguins were two months old. They had lost their fuzz. It was time to jump in the water.

[Penguins are on the edge of the ice, getting ready to jump into the water.]

Mother Penguin 1 and Father Penguin 1: Time to jump in the water.

Mother Penguin 2 and Father Penguin 2: Jump off the ice, Betty and Sammy.

Betty: *[Jumps into the water.]* Whoopee! This is fun.

Sammy: *[Jumps into the water.]* Wow, it's nice and cold.

Mother Penguin 3: Time to jump in the water, Peter.

Father Penguin 3: Follow us, Peter.

Peter: I won't jump. I'm not ready yet! I'll just watch.

[The penguins are swimming and diving. Peter is sitting on the ice watching them.]

Narrator: So the other penguins swam. They dove and leaped.
But Peter just watched on the ice. Then Peter heard a sound.

[The sea lion is on one side of Peter. The penguins are swimming on the other side.]

Sea Lion: Arr, arr.

Peter: What's that? It's a sea lion! Oh, no. No one sees it! Swim for the ice, everyone! A sea lion! A sea lion!

Narrator: But Betty and Sammy did not hear him. The mother and father penguins did not hear him.

Peter: I have to warn them. One . . . two . . . three . . .

[Peter jumps into the water.]

Peter: There's a sea lion! A sea lion! Swim to the ice. Quick!

Narrator: Everyone swam to the ice. The sea lion chased them.
The penguins popped up out of the water. They popped up onto the ice.

[Penguins gather around Peter.]

Betty: You warned us, Peter.

Sammy: You saw the sea lion.

Mother Penguin 3: You jumped in the water!

Father Penguin 3: You saved us!

Everyone: Let's have a party!

Mother Penguin 3: We can eat fish.

Father Penguin 3: We can eat squid.

Peter: I'm not ready yet . . . just kidding!

Narrator: After that day, Peter was always first. The other penguins had to keep up with Peter. He was never last again.

The End

Teacher's Guide

Peter Penguin's Not Ready Yet

Using the Play

While the simple text in this play is appropriate for beginning readers, the many lines and stage directions may be daunting to them. You may wish to copy each actor's lines on a separate piece of paper, and cue each actor when he or she is supposed to speak or move. After a few rehearsals, students should be able to jump right in at the appropriate time. As teacher, you may wish to act as the narrator as well.

Background

Peter Penguin and his friends are Adélie penguins that live in Antarctica. While all 18 species of penguins live below the equator, only the Adélie and the Emperor penguins breed in Antarctica. Other penguins breed in Australia, New Zealand, on the Galapagos Islands, and on other islands in cold southern waters.

Penguins can't fly, but they are great swimmers. They use their wings to swim through the water. In the play, the young penguins had to wait until they lost their fuzz before they could swim. That's because they are born with soft feathers that keep them warm, but these feathers aren't waterproof and can't protect them from the cold water.

Sea lions, sharks, killer whales, and a bird called the skua are all predators that feed on penguins. Penguins, in turn, feed on fish, squid, and small crustaceans called krill.

Book Links

Antarctica by Helen Cowcher (Sunburst, 1991)

Antarctic Antics: A Book of Penguin Poems by Judy Sierra (Harcourt Brace, 1998)

Mr. Popper's Penguins by Richard Atwater and Florence Atwater (Little, Brown and Co., 1938)

Penguin (See How They Grow) by Mary Ling (Dorling Kindersley, 1993)

Penguins by Roger Tory Peterson (Houghton Mifflin, 1979)

Extending the Play

What Happens Next?

The story of Peter Penguin is fun and exciting, and students can learn facts about penguin growth along the way. Try this fun folder activity to review those facts with students, and practice the skill of sequencing at the same time.

Write the following sentences on one side of small index cards. On the back of each card, write the corresponding number:

1 Mother and father penguins keep the eggs warm.

2 The penguin eggs hatch.

3 The penguins learn how to slide on the ice.

4 The penguins lose their fuzz.

5 Betty and Sammy learn how to swim.

6 Peter Penguin sees the sea lion.

7 Peter Penguin jumps into the water.

8 The penguins swim to safety.

Make a small pocket on the front of a manila folder and store the cards there. On the inside of the folder, draw eight rectangles numbered 1-8. To complete the folder activity, students should place the cards on the spaces inside the folder in the proper order.

Students can check the numbers on the backs of the cards to see if they are correct.

Are You Ready Yet?

Although Peter Penguin is a bird, he does have a lot in common with young children, who are often fearful or anxious about trying new things or taking on new challenges. Discuss with students times when they may have felt like Peter Penguin. How did they feel on the first day of school? the first time they tried a new food? the first time they learned how to ride a bicycle? Students can write about their experiences:

The first time I _____

I felt _____.

Now I think that _____.

Feathered Friends

Penguins have many things in common with other birds, but they are also different from other birds. Make a Venn diagram on the board comparing penguins to a bird native to your area. For the diagram, make two interlocking circles. On the left side of the first circle, write down things that are unique to your bird (i.e., lives in California, flies, eats insects); in the center of the interlocking circles, write down things that are common to the two birds (have feathers, lay eggs); and in the right side of the second circle write down things that are unique to penguins (live below the equator, can swim). You may wish to brainstorm these qualities first and then put them in their proper place in the diagram.

How About Bats?

by Carol Pugliano-Martin

Characters

* Bobby Batgood, Game Show Host
* Player #1
* Player #2
* Player #3
* Audience
* Bat #1
* Bat #2
* Bat #3

Props

* Incorrect Answer Buzzer (can be voiced by a student)

Act 1

Bobby: Hello, and welcome to the game show *How About Bats?* We ask questions about bats. Our players try to give us the answers.

[Audience applauds and cheers.]

Bobby: I'm your host, Bobby Batgood. I would like to welcome our three players.

Player #1: Hello, Bobby.

Player #2: It's nice to be here.

Player #3: I can't wait to play.

Bobby: As you know, the purpose of this game is to see what you know about bats. Let's begin. Player Number One, are bats birds?

Player #1: They have wings and they fly, so they must be birds.

[The Incorrect Answer Buzzer buzzes.]

Bobby: No, I'm sorry. Bats are not birds. They are mammals. They do have wings, but they are covered with fur, not feathers. They don't lay eggs like birds do, either. Player Number Two, are bats blind?

Player #2: Yes, Bobby. Bats are blind.

[The Incorrect Answer Buzzer buzzes.]

Bobby: That answer is also not true. Bats can see, but they also use a powerful sense of hearing to find their way around. Player Number Three, it's your turn. Do all bats live in caves?

Player #3: Definitely. They all live in creepy, dark caves.

[The Incorrect Answer Buzzer buzzes.]

Bobby: Wrong. Some bats live in caves. But other bats live in trees or under plants. Some live under bridges or in empty buildings.

Player #3: I didn't know that!

Bobby: Stay tuned for round two of *How About Bats!*

Act 2

Bobby: Welcome back! Now it's time to bring out our very special guest stars. These guests know more about bats than anyone. Please give them a warm welcome.

[The bats enter.]

Player #1: Hey! They're bats!

Bats: Hello, Bobby.

Bobby: Hello, friends. These three folks seem to be confused about bats. I thought you might be able to help them.

Bat #1: Sure, Bobby. Did you folks all know that bats help people?

Player #1: No way. That's impossible.

Bat #1: We do. We eat many, many insects. If we didn't eat them, they might destroy the crops that you humans eat.

Bat #2: Bats also help flowers to grow.

Player #2: What do bats have to do with flowers?

Bat #2: We bring pollen from flower to flower, just like bees. The pollen helps more flowers to grow.

Player #3: Wow. You really do help humans. I thought you just flew around and got tangled in people's hair.

Bat #3: Actually, bats are very shy around people. We would not usually fly close enough to get tangled in hair.

Player #1: This sure has changed my mind about bats.

Player #2: There's so much about bats I didn't know.

Player #3: I'm sorry we misunderstood you.

Bat #1: That's OK. But please go home and tell other people what you've learned.

All Players: We will!

Bobby: Well, thanks for coming on the show.

Player #1: Hey, who won the game?

Bobby: Well, now that you know the truth about bats, you are all winners. Congratulations!

[Audience applauds and cheers.]

The End

Teacher's Guide

How About Bats?

Using the Play

Many teachers have introduced bat themes into their curriculum to help clear up misconceptions about these useful animals. Halloween time is also a great opportunity to use this play, which may help dispel children's fears. (Please note, however, that children should be warned never, ever to touch a bat or any other wild animal. While only a very small percentage of bats are rabies carriers, the threat does exist.)

No set is needed for the play; Bobby Batgood and the three players can stand or sit at the front of the classroom, while seated students can act as the audience.

Background

There are almost 1,000 species of bats in the world. One of the most common species in the U.S. and Canada is the little brown bat, which your students may have seen catching mosquitoes by the light of a streetlamp.

Bats can fly, but they are mammals. They are covered with fur, give birth to live young, and nurse their babies. While bats have these things in common, there are many differences among species. Some bats sleep, or roost, indoors in caves and barns. Others roost outdoors in tree branches. Bats range in size from microbats such as the bumblebee bat, which weighs less than a penny, to megabats such as the flying fox, which has a wingspan of six feet. Contrary to popular belief, all bats do not drink blood. Most microbats eat insects. Fruit makes up the diet of most megabats.

As the play states, no species of bat is blind; however, bats do rely on special senses, such as echolocation, to help them get around in the dark. And bats do eat millions of harmful insects each year, and have been crucial in repollinating the world's rain forests. However, over half of the bats in the

U.S. and Canada are currently threatened and endangered. Scientists and organizations like Bat Conservation International are working hard to save bat populations.

Book Links

Bat Jamboree by Kathi Apelt, illustrated by Melissa Sweet (Morrow Junior Books, 1996)

Bat Time by Ruth Horowitz, illustrated by Susan Avishai (Macmillan Publishing Company, 1991)

Stellaluna by Janell Cannon (Harcourt Brace and Company, 1993)

A Promise to the Sun by Tolowa M. Mallel, illustrated by Beatriz Vidal (Little, Brown, 1992)

Extension Activities

Fact or Fiction

Before introducing the play, asks students to brainstorm a list of things they already know about bats. After the play, review the list with students. Which statements on the list are true? Which statements on the list are false? Use the statements from the list, along with additional information from the play and other sources, to create a bat flash-card game. Write a statement on one side of an index card, and on the other, write the word "FACT" or "FICTION." Students can use the cards to quiz one another on their knowledge of bat facts.

Bats Around the World

If your students enjoy learning about the many different species of bats, they may also enjoy finding out where those bats live. First, research (as a class or as an assignment) some popular bats and their locations. For example:

Vampire bat: Mexico, Central America, South America

Little brown bat: U.S. and Canada

Bumblebee bat: Thailand

Pipistrelle: North America

Flying fox: Asia, Australia

Mexican free-tailed bats: Mexico, U.S.

To create a "Bats Around the World" bulletin board, start with a world map. Have students draw or copy pictures of the bats they've researched and write the names of the bats on the pictures. Invite students to come up to the board and tack each bat to an area that the bat calls home.

Commercial Break

The time between Act 1 and Act 2 would be a great place for your students to insert a "commercial" into the game show. Invite groups of students to write and perform a commercial that gives information about bats. For example, they may choose to write a public service announcement with the theme "Be Kind to Bats." Another commercial may pitch a vacation package for a tour of bats around the world. Students can perform their commercials during a performance of the play.

Take Your Time, Tadpole

by Tracey West

Characters

* Storyteller 1
* Storyteller 2
* Tadpole/Young Frog
* Turtle
* Frog 1
* Frog 2
* Minnow
* Snake
* Dragonfly

Act 1

A pond. Frog 1, Frog 2, Minnow, Dragonfly, and Turtle are gathered around frog eggs in the water.

Storyteller 1: It was a sunny spring day at Frog Pond.

Storyteller 2: A mother frog had just laid her eggs.

Storyteller 1: Some of the animals in the pond saw the eggs.

Frog 1: Look at those eggs!

Frog 2: They're just lying there, covered in jelly.

Frog 1: They could be hopping around, like us!

[Frog 1 and Frog 2 hop around.]

Dragonfly: Flying is better! *[Flies in a circle.]*

Minnow: They can't even swim yet. *[Swims.]*

Turtle: *[To eggs.]* Take your time, eggs. Soon they will see what you can do.

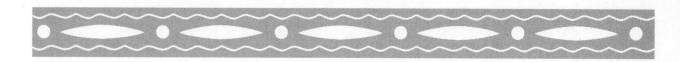

Act 2

Storyteller 1: In about ten days, the eggs hatched.

Storyteller 2: Soon thousands of tadpoles swam out into the pond water.

Storyteller 1: One tadpole stayed behind.

Tadpole: Hi, everybody!

Frog 1: Look at the little tadpole.

Frog 2: What good are you? You can't even hop.

Dragonfly: No! You don't have legs.

Tadpole: [Sadly.] I guess you're right.

Minnow: That's OK, tadpole. You can swim with me. You can use your tail.

Turtle: And you can use your gills to breathe underwater.

Frog 1: Big deal.

Frog 2: We can swim, too, you know.

Tadpole: I wish I could hop!

Turtle: Take your time, Tadpole. Soon they will see what you can do.

Act 3

Storyteller 1: The weather got warmer.

Storyteller 2: Tadpole ate and ate. It grew and grew.

Tadpole: Look, everybody! I have tiny back legs now. And tiny front legs, too.

Frog 1: Big deal.

Frog 2: They're still not as strong as our legs.

Frog 1: And you still have your tail.

Frog 2: And you still have your gills.

Dragonfly: *[Flies in.]* Look out, everybody! Snake is coming!

Frog 1: *[Hops.]* I'm out of here!

Frog 2: *[Hops.]* Me too!

Storyteller 1: Snake crawled to the pond's edge.

Tadpole: Turtle! I can't hop! What will I do? Snake will eat me.

Turtle: Don't worry, Tadpole. You are the same color as the leaves floating

on the pond. Hide among the leaves.

[Tadpole swims away.]

Storyteller 2: Tadpole hid among the leaves.

Storyteller 1: Snake did not see Tadpole.

Storyteller 2: Snake crawled away.

[Snake crawls away. Tadpole swims back.]

Tadpole: Thanks, Turtle. But I still wish I could have hopped away like the frogs.

Turtle: Take your time, Tadpole. Soon you will see what you can do.

Act 4

Storyteller 1: Tadpole's legs got longer and stronger.

Storyteller 2: Tadpole's tail disappeared.

Storyteller 1: Tadpole's gills disappeared.

Storyteller 2: Now Tadpole breathed with lungs instead.

Storyteller 1: Tadpole was now a young frog!

Young Frog: Look at me! I have strong legs. I have webbed feet.

Turtle: You can hop on land now.

Minnow: Will you still swim with me?

Young Frog: Sure I will.

Dragonfly: You're a frog now.

Frog 1: You don't have to swim with Minnow.

Frog 2: You can hop with us.

Young Frog: Dragonfly, do you know what else I have?

Dragonfly: What's that?

Young Frog: I have a long sticky tongue. It's perfect for catching yummy dragonflies! *[Hops after dragonfly.]*

Dragonfly: Time for me to fly! *[Flies away.]*

Frog 1: That was funny, kid.

Frog 2: Yup. Why don't you come hopping with us?

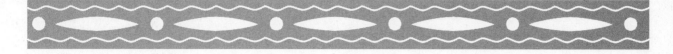

Young Frog: Not right now. I think I'll stay here with Turtle for awhile.

Frog 1: Whatever you say.

[Frog 1 and Frog 2 hop away.]

Turtle: You don't have to stay here with me.

Young Frog: I want to. Besides, I'm not in a hurry. I have plenty of time. Right?

Turtle: *[Smiles.]* That's right, Young Frog.

The End

Teacher's Guide

Take Your Time, Tadpole

Using the Play

To provide a speaking role for every student in your class, you can easily divide the storytellers' lines among a larger group of students. Students can stand in a group on one side of the stage, and step forward when it is their turn to speak. Tadpole and Young Frog can be played by two different actors. In addition, you'll notice that no gender has been assigned to the characters. Each role can be played by either a boy or a girl.

In Act 1, you may choose to have several actors curled up into balls, pretending to be frog eggs. In Act 2, those characters can "hatch" and swim away, while Tadpole stays behind.

Background

This play shows the transformation, or metamorphosis, of a tadpole into a frog. This transformation begins in spring, when a female frog lays thousands of tiny round eggs in the water. The eggs are held together by a thick jelly. When the eggs hatch, the tadpoles cling to the jelly, eating some of it and gaining strength. As they grow stronger, they will swim and swim, eating algae and extracting oxygen from the water with their feathery gills.

The complete transformation from tadpole to frog can take anywhere from two weeks to two years, depending on the species. During this time, the tadpole's long tail will gradually be absorbed by the tadpole's body as it is replaced by two strong back legs and two front legs. The gills will also be absorbed as the frog's lungs and nostrils develop. The nutrients in the gills and tail are recycled by the frog's body.

When fully formed, frogs have some amazing features, too. They don't drink water, but absorb it through their skin. Webbed feet help them swim. Powerful hind legs allow them to jump great lengths and travel at fast speeds. A long sticky tongue flicks out to catch and trap insects.

Book Links

Fish Is Fish by Leo Lionni (Alfred A. Knopf, 1987)

From Tadpole to Frog by Wendy Pfeffer (HarperCollins, 1994)

Pond Year by Kathryn Lasky (Candlewick Press, 1997)

Tale of a Tadpole by Barbara Ann Porte (Orchard Books, 1997)

Extending the Play

Changes, Changes

You can use the story of Tadpole to discuss the changes in your own students' lives. Discuss how the character of Tadpole might feel when the other frogs and the dragonfly tease it about not being able to hop. Ask students if they have older brothers, sisters, cousins, or older friends. What are some things the older kids can do that they can't do yet? How do they feel about that? Remind them of Turtle's advice—to take your time. Do they think this is good advice?

Leaping Lily Pads!

You can use a frog theme to create an interactive activity to match your curriculum any time of year. To make the game, cut out 20 lily pads from green construction paper. Then draw a frog on white paper, photocopy it 20 times, and cut it out.

On each frog, write a question or fact. On each lily pad, write the matching answer. For example:

Science: animals/animal babies
Language Arts: synonyms/antonyms
Math: math fact/answer
Social Studies: states/state capitals

Use a bulletin board as a game board. Staple the lily pads to the bulletin board. Put all of the frogs in a "pond" or box. To play, each player must pick a frog from the box, then match the frog to its lily pad, attaching it with a tack. The game is over when all of the frogs are on their matching lily pads.

A Classroom Pond

Students sometimes bring tadpoles or frog eggs to class. To turn this into a learning experience, fill a small aquarium with pond water, pond mud, and rocks. Make sure some of the rocks are above water. Put the tadpoles and/or eggs in the water.

Keep the aquarium at room temperature (about 62 to 72 degrees Fahrenheit). Then observe the tadpoles. Ask students: *What will the tadpoles eat?* (the tiny plants in the pond water and mud; add more pond water and muck as the tadpoles grow) *After they turn into frogs, how can we make sure that the frogs have air to breathe?* (by making sure the rocks are above water) When your tadpoles become frogs, you will need to feed them insects, such as meal worms and flies. Consider releasing them back into the wild before they mature or soon after.

Adapted from A Year of Hands-on Science *by Lynne Kepler (Scholastic Professional Books, 1996)*

The Ocean Olympics

by Stephanie Lesser

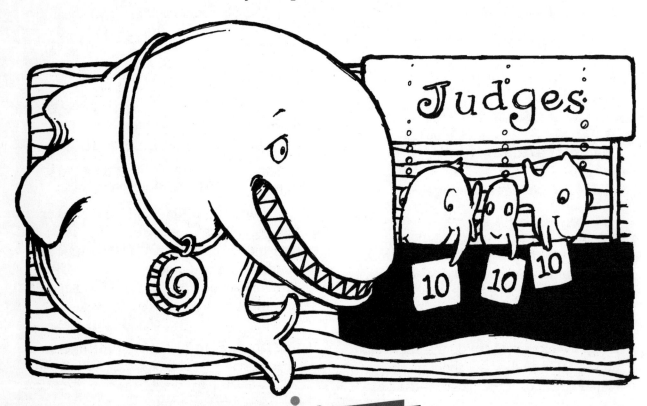

Act 1

It's very early on a sunny summer morning, along a giant colorful coral reef.

Narrator: Sharks are meeting near the Great Barrier Reef along the coast of Australia. They've come from all over the world to compete in the shark events at the Ocean Olympics. But before they swim the rest of the way, some sharks are talking about who the winners will be.

Howard: *[Swinging his head from side to side.]* I'm a hammerhead and I think I'll win. With a nose like this, I can smell really well! Who else has a nose as fine as mine?

Timothy: Can't you see the winner will be me—the thresher shark! I have the longest, strongest tail you'll ever see!

Garrett: *[Showing his teeth.]* Well, I say I'll win something. With my hundreds of big sharp teeth, there couldn't be a greater choice than me— the great white, the *greatest* hunter in the sea!

William: *[Slowly swimming around.]* True, Garrett, you are a great hunter. Thomas and Timothy are great hunters, too. Anyway, there are hundreds of kinds of sharks, and we all have rows and rows and rows of teeth.

Howard: You're not the only one with big sharp teeth, Garrett!

Margie: What about me? I'm the mako—the fastest shark of all—and I always win the race!

Selma: I'm the swell shark, and the *swell* choice! Who else do you know that can swallow enough water to *triple* in size? Nobody can scare away attackers like I can.

Tommy: *[To Selma.]* Even tripled, you're not big enough to scare me. I'm tough. I'm one of the biggest sharks in the sea, too. Of course, none of us are as big as William!

Garrett: Hey, William, which one of us do you think will win?

William: I think that we're all special. Besides, all sharks are winners. Way back, when all the dinosaurs lived and died, we stuck around! A lot of fish didn't make it.

Margie: *[Racing off.]* I'm not about to stick around here and miss my chance to win. Come on, let's go!

[The sharks swim away to the Olympic arena.]

Act 2

The shark events are finished. The judges are huddled on the ocean floor, talking to each other as the sharks slowly swim around in front of them.

Judge 1: There are entirely too many sharks here! They're scaring away some of the other contestants!

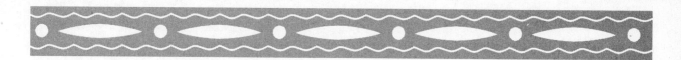

Judge 2: That's why we always have the shark awards first—so they can leave first.

Judge 3: We still have to decide which shark should come in first place.

Judge 1: *[To other Judges.]* Well, the sharks are about to swim by us again. Maybe then we can decide which shark deserves the gold medal.

Judge 2: *Attention!* Calling all sharks! At this time, all sharks please swim past the judges one more time.

Narrator: Just then, the sharks spotted some fishing boats in the distance. The boats were loaded with nets and lines.

Margie: Fishing boats! They're a shark's worst enemy. Time for me to make a quick getaway! *[Swims away.]*

Selma: Gulp! *[Swallows water.]*

Garrett: Let me at them! *[Bares his teeth.]* I'd like to scare them away!

Tommy: Those boats are even bigger than I am! If we're going to scare them off, we'll need more sharks. I'm going to find some! *[He swims off.]*

William: I'm a little scared. But I am the biggest shark here. Maybe there's something I can do to help. *[He swims up to the boats].*

Narrator: William swam between the crowds of fish and the boats, protecting everyone at the Olympics. It didn't take long for the fishers to see that the big spotted whale shark would not let them near the rest of the animals. The boats turned and sailed away.

[The sharks swim back to the judging area.]

Judge 1: *[To other Judges.]* Well, Judges—I think we know which shark deserves first place. Let's announce the winners!

Judge 2: *[To everyone.]* We hereby declare the winners: The medal for Speediest Shark goes to Mako Shark Margie.

Margie: *[Quickly grabs her award, then swims away.]* I've got the fastest fins in the sea!

Judge 3: The medal for the Strongest Jaw goes to Great White Garrett.

Garrett: *[Opens mouth wide.]* I'm an eating machine!

Judge 1: The medal for Best Sense of Smell goes to Hammerhead Howard.

Howard: *[Sniffs loudly].* I smell victory!

Judge 2: The medal for Best Way to Scare Off Attackers goes to Swell Shark Selma.

Selma: *[Puffs up.]* I'm swelling with pride!

Judge 3: The medal for Toughest Shark goes to Tiger Shark Tommy.

Tommy: *[Looks mean].* I'm big and I'm bad!

Judge 1: The medal for the Strongest Tail goes to Thresher Timothy.

Timothy: *[Swishes tail.]* I guess this is the *end* of the awards.

Judge 1: Not yet. In first place, overall, the winner is . . . the bravest, biggest shark in the sea! Congratulations to Whale Shark William! And thank you, William, for saving us. You're a true hero!

[All the sharks circle around William and cheer for him.]

Tommy: Grrreat job, William!

Margie: Good for you, William! I guess nice sharks really do finish first!

Timothy: Thanks, William, you really are the bravest shark in the sea!

William: Thanks!

Selma: We should celebrate! Let's get a bite to eat.

Judge 2: That's a good idea. But could you do us a favor?

All Sharks: What?

Judge 3: Please don't eat any of the contestants!

[All the sharks laugh and swim away.]

The End

Teacher's Guide

The Ocean Olympics

Using the Play

Your students will enjoy creating a colorful backdrop for the set. This play is set in the ocean near a coral reef, so ask students to research ocean animals and other life that can be found in a reef. With their research to guide them, let their creativity run wild with paints, crayons, and markers on a large roll of paper, or large sheets of posterboard connected together. (You can also use an old bedsheet and fabric paints, if available.)

Background

Sharks live in all oceans and are often solitary, but some species swim in large schools. Scientists have observed more than four species and over a hundred individuals feeding together. Some shark species migrate or hunt in enormous groups of a thousand or more individuals.

The sharks in the play seem to like bragging about themselves. Here's a little more information about the shark facts in the play:

* **Whale shark:** At 45 feet long, the whale shark is the largest shark in the world.

* **Hammerhead shark:** All sharks have an excellent sense of smell. The hammerhead can smell blood from more than a mile away!

* **Mako shark:** This shark's amazing speed and agility make it a fierce predator. It can feed on dolphins, porpoise, and other sharks.

* **Tiger shark:** Another big shark, the tiger shark has reached lengths of 21 feet.

* **Thresher shark:** This shark's tail fin is nearly as long as the rest of its body. It uses its long tail to stun fish; the scared fish form a group, and that means easy feeding for the thresher.

* **Great white shark:** This shark's face is built for eating: When its jaws open, its mouth moves to the front, and its snout bends back and out of the way.

* **Swell shark:** These sharks can fill up their stomachs with air or water to make themselves look larger. Inflated, the shark can scare away attackers and lodge itself between rocks so that it can't be removed.

Book Links

Punia and the King of Sharks, a Hawaiian Folktale adapted by Lee Wardlaw (Dial Books for Young Readers, 1993)

Questions and Answers About Sharks by Ann McGovern (Scholastic Trade, 1995)

A Sea Full of Sharks by Betsy Maestro (Scholastic Trade, 1997)

Sharks in the Sea by Seymour Simon (HarperCollins Juvenile Books, 1995)

Extending the Play

Ocean Food Chain

The medal-winning qualities possessed by sharks in this play make them efficient predators. In the ocean food chain, sharks are usually at the top. Have children make three-link ocean food chains using plants and animals that can be found in the ocean (or more specifically, along a coral reef).

You can challenge children to do their own research, or provide the information and have children make connections: Draw or paste pictures of ocean animals or plants on individual index cards. Punch a hole in the top and bottom of each card. Put the cards at a learning center, along with small lengths of string or yarn. Instruct students to link three cards together that form a food chain. A sample food chain can be algae (bottom), parrotfish (middle), and lemon shark (top).

Shark Q & A

Make a class big book titled "Questions and Answers About Sharks." Write a number of questions on sheets of chart paper. Questions may include:

What do sharks eat?

Where do sharks live?

How do sharks catch prey?

What is the biggest shark in the world?

What is the smallest shark in the world?

For more ideas, see the book *Questions and Answers About Sharks* by Ann McGovern.

Divide the class into groups and assign a page to each group. Students should research the question, write out the answer, and illustrate the page. When all the pages are complete, bind them together to make your finished book.

Bella's Summer Picnic

by Robin Bernard

Act 1

A bright sunny day in the park. Bella Butterfly flutters onstage.

Bella Butterfly: *[To herself.]* What a super-duper day for a picnic! It's warm, it's sunny, and all my guests will *love* dining on these wonderful bluebells!

Albert Ant: *[Entering.]* Well, Bella, here I am! You certainly picked a great day for a picnic!

Bella Butterfly: Oh, Albert, I'm so glad you could make it! And you're the very first guest to arrive. But you can start eating right now. Just help yourself. There's plenty of bluebell nectar for everybody!

Albert Ant: Nectar? That's very sweet of you, Bella, but I'm an ant, remember? I can't sip nectar like you do.

Bella Butterfly: Oh, Albert, I'm *sooo* sorry. I forgot you don't have a built-in straw!

Albert: Don't give it another thought, Bella. I'll have a little fungus snack when I get home. Hey, look—here comes Gus!

Gus Grasshopper: Hello, Albert. Greetings, Bella! So? *[Looking around.]* Where's the picnic food?

Bella Butterfly: Right here, Gus. *[Pointing to the flowers.]* A buffet picnic

feast of sweet bluebell nectar.

Gus Grasshopper: *[Shaking his head.]* Not for me, thanks. I need my green veggies. Besides, Bella, I'm a grasshopper, and I don't have a straw like you do.

Bella Butterfly: I'm so sorry, Gus, I forgot! Oh, look! Here comes Betty. Maybe she'll want some sweet nectar.

Betty Beetle: *[Enters in a rush, catching her breath.]* Sorry I'm late, guys, and am I starved! What's to eat?

Bella Butterfly: There's some yummy bluebell nectar, Betty. And I'm glad you're so hungry, because Albert and Gus can't eat nectar and there's so much of it!

Betty Beetle: *[Gesturing "no" with her front legs.]* Not me either, Bella. I like my food a little meatier. Besides, I don't have a straw!

Bella Butterfly: *[Holding her head in her hands.]* Oh, dear, oh dear. What an awful hostess I turned out to be! I forgot what my friends can eat and now they'll all go away hungry.

Freddy Flea: *[Hopping in.]* Heeeere's Freddy! Just hopped over to join in the picnic. So where's the blood?

Bella Butterfly: I'm sorry, Freddy, I really goofed. There *is* no blood at this picnic, only nectar. I forgot that you like blood. And I forgot what all my other friends like to eat, too. My picnic is a great big flop!

Margo Mosquito: *[Enters humming.]* Hello, hello, hello! Oh, am I full! *[Patting her belly.]* Hey! What's wrong? Why do you look so sad, Bella?

Bella Butterfly: Because I *am* sad, Margo. My picnic is a *disaster!* I don't have the right food for my guests and . . .

Margo Mosquito: Now, now, Bella. Not to worry. I just finished a great meal! And if we move the picnic to the other side of the field, all of your guests can have a *feast.* Come on, I'll show you!

[Bella and her guests follow Margo Mosquito.]

Act 2

The remains of a "people" picnic are spread out on a paper tablecloth on the grass. Mom and daughter are playing checkers while dad and son are playing Frisbee with their dog.

Margo Mosquito: *[Pointing to the leftover food on the tablecloth.]* I ask you, is this a feast, or what?

Albert Ant: I'll say! Look at all these cookie crumbs! Excellent!

Gus Grasshopper: Cool! Here's my favorite green salad! These people have great taste!

Betty Beetle: Look! Barbecued chicken! Hamburgers! What a terrific menu!

Freddy Flea: *[Pointing to the dog.]* Aha! Here comes my favorite snack, wagging its tail. Excuse me, folks, I'll jump on for a little appetizer and catch you later.

Bella Butterfly: Margo, I can't thank you enough! You've saved my picnic party! Now why don't you have a bite to eat?

Margo Mosquito *[Laughing.]* No, thanks, I've had my dinner, Bella. Take a peek at the checker players, and you'll know why I'm so full!

[All of them turn to look at the checker players. Mom is scratching her arms, and the daughter is scratching her leg. All the insects exit, chuckling quietly.]

The End

Teacher's Guide

Bella's Summer Picnic

Using the Play

The big stars of this play are the insect characters. You may wish to make simple costumes by making paper headbands with pipe-cleaner "antennae" attached. You can also take it further by having students research their insect roles and create appropriate costumes by adding things like wings and extra legs, or they could take the simple step of dressing in the appropriate color.

Background

In this play, students learn about the mouth parts and feeding habits of these insects:

Butterflies: There are thousands of species of butterflies in the world, and many of them are brightly colored. The "built-in straw" that Bella has is a long tube called a proboscis. Butterflies use this to sip nectar from flowers such as phlox, Joe-Pye weed, and dandelions.

Ants: Fungus-eating ants, such as Albert, gather green leaves, and then grow fungus on the leaves in underground tunnels. Other kinds of ants eat seeds, sweet foods, and even other insects.

Beetles: There are more than 250,000 species of beetles in the world, and many of those species eat plant parts. Some beetles, like Betty, feed on dead plant or animal material, and other kinds of beetles eat other insects.

Grasshoppers: These insects are voracious eaters of vegetable matter, which sometimes makes them pests to farmers. They also rely on plants to provide shelter.

Fleas: These wingless insects have piercing mouth parts that help them suck blood. They feed on warm-blooded animals, such as rats, chickens, and of course, dogs.

Mosquitoes: Like butterflies, mosquitoes also have a proboscis, and male and female mosquitoes use them to suck flower nectar. However, adult females also use their syringe-like proboscis to suck blood from humans and animals. They need the blood in order to produce eggs.

Book Links

Amazing Insects (Eyewitness Juniors, No. 26) by Laurence A. Mound (Knopf, 1993)

Backyard Bugs by Robin Kittrell Laughlin (Chronicle Books, 1996)

Bugs, Beetles, and Butterflies by Harriet Ziefert (Puffin, 1998)

Miss Spider's Tea Party by David Kirk (Scholastic Press, 1994)

Extending the Play

A Class Picnic

Your class can have a picnic just like Bella Butterfly's. Assign a different kind of insect to each student in your class. Have students research their insect and draw a picture of that insect's favorite food to bring to the picnic. At your bug picnic, students can sit in a circle or in groups on a blanket on the floor and "share" their food by talking about what they know about their insect and what it eats. To take this a step further, have students create insect costumes to wear to the picnic.

If you hold your picnic outdoors, you could add a bug hunt to the festivities. Invite students to search for real insects in your picnic area. When you're back indoors, record what you found on the chalkboard or on poster paper.

Helpful or Harmful

We call some insects "pests" because they damage crops, spread disease, and make us itch. Other insects are very beneficial to humans because they help pollinate flowers, aerate the soil, or because they eat harmful insects.

Have students make insect fact cards on index cards. On one side of the card, students can draw a picture of an insect. On the other, they can list facts about the insect. Students should find out whether their insects are helpful or harmful.

You can use these cards in many ways:

• Create a Helpful/Harmful bulletin board. Attach the helpful insects to one side of the board, and the harmful insects to the other side.

• Challenge the students to sort the cards into helpful/harmful piles without looking at the information on the back. They can also sort the cards in other ways: by diet, whether or not they have wings, etc.

Further Adventures

Use these story titles to inspire students to write more adventures for the bug buddies in this play. Encourage students to add new bug facts that are appropriate to the story.

"When Bella Butterfly Was a Baby"

"Betty Beetle Goes to School"

"Gus Grasshopper Wins the Game"

"Freddy Flea's First Bite"

"Margo Mosquito Takes a Trip"

"Albert Ant Goes to Work"

Dinosaurs With a Difference

by Paula Thomas

APATOSAURUS

Characters

* Teacher
* Michelle
* Tony
* Crystal
* Jacob
* Kevin
* Carmen
* Apatosaurus #1
* Apatosaurus #2
* Acrocanthosaurus
* Styracosaurus
* Deinonychus
* Parasaurolophus
* Euoplocephalus

Props

* a sign with each dinosaur's name written on it

Act 1

A classroom. The children are seated on the rug listening to a student read a story.

Michelle: . . . and so that is what I think life was like when the dinosaurs lived on the earth. The End.

[All clap.]

Teacher: That was an excellent story, Michelle. Does anyone have any questions or comments for Michelle?

Tony: Where did you learn all that stuff about dinosaurs?

Michelle: My mom and dad took me to that new Natural History Museum. It has this really cool dinosaur exhibit.

Crystal: Isn't that where we're going tomorrow on our field trip?

Teacher: *[Smiling.]* Yes, it is.

Jacob: I can't wait. Dinosaurs are awesome.

Crystal: I think so, too. In fact, I think we should have a dinosaur as our class mascot.

Tony: A mascot? You mean like a symbol of our class, like you see on signs and hats and T-shirts and stuff?

Teacher: That's right, Tony. You know class, Crystal has a good idea. When we go to the museum tomorrow, try to decide which dinosaur would make the best mascot for our class.

Children: *[Talking excitedly.]* Yes! That would be great!

Act 2

The next day, the students enter a museum hall. There are large models of dinosaurs on display.

Teacher: I'll be right back, students. I need to find the museum guide. While I'm gone, try to find out what you can about these dinosaurs. I think you'll be surprised. *[Winks at audience]*.

Michelle: Surprised? I wonder what she means by that?

Apatosaurus #1: I don't know. There are never many surprises around here.

[Children react with shock.]

Carmen: A talking dinosaur! This is colossal. This is stupendous. This is amazing. This is . . .

Crystal: *[Suspicious.]* There must be some kind of trick to it.

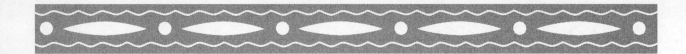

Apatosaurus #2: Not really. It gets lonely being on display all day. It's nice to have someone to talk to.

Children: [*Looking at each other.*] Wow!

Kevin: [*Raising his hand, asks timidly.*] You're not going to eat us, are you? Aren't a lot of dinosaurs ca-ca-car . . .

Crystal: Carnivores are what you call meat-eating dinosaurs, Kevin. And omnivores eat meat and plants.

Tony: Whatever you call it, that spells danger to me!

Apatosaurus #1: Don't worry! My friend and I are plant-eaters. And the other dinosaurs won't hurt you, either.

Michelle: Then maybe you can help us. We're trying to decide which dinosaur would make the best mascot for our class.

Apatosaurus #2: Hmm. I'm not sure. Maybe you could talk to the other dinosaurs and ask them.

Jacob: That sounds like a plan! Let's go!

Kevin: Are you sure we won't get eaten?

All: Kevin!

[*The students form groups and walk off.*]

Act 3

[Michelle, Carmen, and Tony walk to one side of the exhibit. There they see Acrocanthosaurus and Styracosaurus.]

Tony: Check out these guys! They'd make great mascots! Let's go and talk to them.

Michelle: *[Approaches Acrocanthosaurus.]* Excuse me, we are looking for a dinosaur to be our class mascot. Who are you?

Acrocanthosaurus: My name is Acrocanthosaurus. That means "very spiny lizard." If you are looking for a spiny mascot, you need look no further!

Carmen: Wow! How long are those spines going down your back?

Acrocanthosaurus: *[Proudly looks down its back.]* Some of the longest ones are twelve inches long!

Tony: I saw a porcupine once, but its spines were nothing compared to yours.

Carmen: We will definitely tell our class about your stupendous spines!

Michelle: *[Approaches Styracosaurus.]* I know who you are. You're Styracosaurus.

Styracosaurus: Styracosaurus, at your service. If it's easier for you to remember, you can just call me "spiked lizard."

Tony: I can see why. You have long spikes, short spikes, and even a spiky nose horn.

Styracosaurus: I just love spikes!

Carmen: Those spikes sure are super. I think it would be fabulous to have a mascot with all those spikes!

Styracosaurus: Thanks! I'd be honored to be your mascot. But there are so many more dinosaurs to see.

Act 4

Crystal, Jacob, and Kevin walk to the other side of the exhibit area. Now Euoplocephalus , Parasaurolophus, and Deinonychus are standing in the exhibit.

Jacob: We've seen some cool dinosaurs, but these look really strange!

Crystal: This whole day is strange! But I guess it can't hurt to talk to these guys.

Kevin: Are you sure about that? *[Points to Deinonychus.]* This one looks really scary!

Deinonychus: To be sure, if I were a real dinosaur you would have a lot to be afraid of. People call me Deinonychus or "terrible claw." *[Holding up his front foot.]* Can you see why?

Kevin: Yikes! Are those claws as sharp as they look?

Deinonychus: Absolutely! By using my claws and my seventy deadly teeth, I could make a meal out of another dinosaur in no time.

Kevin: *[To Crystal and Jacob.]* I think we've learned enough from this one.

Jacob: *[Approaches the Parasaurolophus.]* What's that on your head?

Crystal: That's a Parasaurolophus, silly. That's a crest on top of its head.

Parasaurolophus: The crest is about five feet long.

Jacob: Wow! What's it for?

Parasaurolophus: It's helpful to push branches and leaves out of my way.

Euoplocephalus: Yes, we all had some pretty useful features. Can you guess what mine is? *[Turns around in a circle.]*

Jacob: Hey, nice tail!

Crystal: What do you expect from a Euoplocephalus?

Euoplocephalus: That is my tail club. When I start swinging it everyone

gets out of my way! *[Starts swinging his tail from side to side].*

Kevin: Yikes! Let's get out of here!

[Kevin runs off. Jacob and Crystal follow, shaking their heads.]

Act 5

Students are all gathered back at the front of the exhibit.

Michelle: Well, does anyone have any ideas about who should be our mascot?

Carmen: We met Acrocanthosaurus. He would be a great mascot. He had spectacular spines that were twelve inches long.

Tony: Don't forget Styracosaurus. What an awesome nose horn!

Kevin: Did you guys meet Deinonychus? He had these huge claws. *[Shivers in fear.]*

Crystal: I prefer Parasaurolophus and his crest.

Jacob: But Euoplocephalus had that cool tail club!

Teacher: *[Enters.]* Hi, everybody. Did you enjoy the exhibit?

Carmen: It was fabulous! Incredible!

Kevin: I'm just glad we didn't get eaten.

All: Kevin!

Teacher: So, did you decide which dinosaur should be our mascot?

Michelle: Well, I don't really think that we can. I think that they were all great.

Jacob: Let's make them all mascots!

Crystal: That seems fair. Who said that we can only choose one?

All: [*High-fiving each other.*] Hooray! Hooray! The dinosaurs have made our day!

The End

Teacher's Guide

Dinosaurs With a Difference

Using the Play

Don't worry about needing a big space for the dinosaur museum; between Act 1 and Act 2, your classroom can quickly be transformed into a dinosaur exhibit hall as the dinosaur actors take their places at the front of the room.

To help set the scene, as well as to assist students in repeating dinosaur names, have students create a name sign for each dinosaur. To extend the activity, students can create a display card for each dinosaur with extra factual information, such as those you might find in a museum display.

Background

This play highlights some fascinating and unusual dinosaurs that children might not be familiar with. These dinosaurs all lived in North America during the Cretaceous period. Here's what else the play doesn't tell you about these dynamic dinos:

* **Acrocanthosaurus** [ak-row-kan-thow-SAWR-us]: This large meat-eater grew to about 40 feet long, and the spines on its back were a foot long.

* **Styracosaurus** [sty-rak-o-SAWR-us]: This plant-eater was about 18 feet long. The six long spines on the back of its neck were made of bone.

* **Deinonychus** [dye-NON-ik-us]: First discovered in the 1960s, this dinosaur is a relative of the Velociraptor. It used its heavy claws and powerful muscles to rip apart prey.

* **Parasaurolophus** [pa-ra-sawr-OL-off-us]: This strange-looking dinosaur is part of the duck-billed dinosaur family. Some scientists think it may have used its six-foot crest to make a honking noise.

* **Euoplocephalus** [you-oh-ploh-SEF-uh-luss]: This dinosaur's skin was covered with plates of bony armor. That, along with its spikes, kept this plant-eater safe from predators.

Book Links

Digging Up Dinosaurs by Aliki (HarperTrophy, 1988)

Dinosaurs: The Fastest, The Fiercest, The Most Amazing by Elizabeth MacLeod (Puffin, 1997)

Dinosaurs: The Very Latest Information and Hands-on Activities from the Museum of the Rockies by Liza Charlesworth and Bonnie Satchabello-Sawyer (Scholastic, 1995)

Extending the Play

Interview With a Dinosaur

In the play, students get to actually talk with dinosaurs. Ask students to imagine that they can talk with a dinosaur. What kind of dinosaur do they want to talk with? What kinds of questions will they ask it? Have students write out their questions.

Challenge students to find out the answers to as many questions as they can on their own. When they've done their research, ask students to imagine that they are the dinosaur. Pair up students and have them interview one another.

Vote for a Mascot

What kind of dinosaur would make the best mascot for your class? Hold a "Mascot Election" to find out.

To begin, divide the class into small groups. Each group should pick one dinosaur that they think would be a good mascot. Instruct the group to find out as much about the dinosaur as they can.

Hold a "Mascot Election" week. Allow students to decorate the room with posters designed to persuade others to vote for their dinosaur. On each day of the week, invite one group to give a speech supporting their dinosaur.

To avoid having a tie when students vote for their dinosaur, hold a preliminary election. Ask each student to vote for two dinosaurs on a ballot. The results of this election should narrow the playing field to two dinosaurs. Hold more speeches before the final vote is cast. Have students tally up the vote. The winning dinosaur is your new class mascot!

Dinosaur Time Line

Dinosaurs lived during the Mesozoic era, 245–65 million years ago. This era is divided into three time periods: the Triassic period (245–208 million years ago), the Jurassic period (208–144 million years ago), and the Cretaceous period (144–66 million years ago).

Use this information to make a simple time line out of three sheets of chart paper. Write the name of the time period on each sheet. Have students fill in the rest of the time line by drawing pictures of dinosaurs and then attaching them to the correct time period.

The Mayflower

by Jane Manners

Characters

* Narrator
* Sam
* Mom
* Dad
* Joseph
* Elizabeth
* John
* Mary
* Sailor #1
* Sailor #2

Props

* a blanket for Sam's "bed"
* handheld video game (could be made from a small box)
* piece of bread (hardtack)

Act 1

Sam is in his bedroom playing a handheld video game.

Narrator: This is Sam Dudley. He is sad. Tomorrow morning he and his parents are moving far away. Sam does not want to move.

[Sam's parents enter, and Sam puts down his video game.]

Mom: Sleep well, Sam. We have to get up early in the morning.

Sam: *[Standing.]* No, we don't.

Mom: Why is that?

Sam: Because I don't want to move. I'm not moving! *[Sitting back down on the bed.]* The trip will be too long. The trip will be too hard.

Dad: Now, Sam, we've been through this before. Mom has a new job.

Sam: What if we move and then we find out we don't like it there?

Mom: Did you know that the Pilgrims probably asked the same questions when they set sail for the New World?

Sam: The Pilgrims?

Dad: That's right. The Pilgrims traveled far from home to start a new life.

Just like us. Now get some sleep.

Sam: *[Getting into bed.]* Wow! We're like the Pilgrims.

Narrator enters while Sam's parents tuck him in for the night and exit. Sam curls up in bed and falls asleep.

Act 2

Narrator: That night Sam had a dream that he was a Pilgrim. In his dream he went back to the year 1620. This was the year when the Pilgrims set out on their long journey across the Atlantic on a ship called the *Mayflower*. There were many children on the ship who, like Sam, were moving far from home.

[Joseph, Mary, Elizabeth, and John enter. Sam wakes up and sleepwalks on board the Mayflower.*]*

Sam: Where am I?

Joseph: You're on the *Mayflower.*

Elizabeth: We're moving to the New World.

John: We've been sailing for sixty-five days.

Sam: Sixty-five days? That's more than two months! How many people are

on the *Mayflower?*

Mary: There are more than one hundred of us.

Sam: More than one hundred? On this tiny ship? It must be crowded.

John: It is. This ship was never meant to carry more than twelve people. It's a cargo ship.

Sam: A cargo ship? Does that mean there's no swimming pool? No game room?

Elizabeth: I'm not sure what you mean, but if you're talking about playing games, we can't do much of that. We had to leave our toys at home.

Sam: No toys?

Joseph: There is no room on the ship. We had to bring important things, like furniture and tools.

Mary: *[Pulling a piece of old bread from her pocket.]* Look what I have! Hardtack!

Sam: That looks like a stale, old piece of bread. Who would want to eat that?

Everyone looks at the bread, then suddenly, each kid grabs a piece and gobbles it up. Sam is surprised by what he sees.

Sam: *[To audience.]* Yuck!

John: It's not so bad. We get to eat other stuff, too, like cheese and beans and salted pork.

Sam: I don't know about this. No toys, a crowded boat, and hard bread to eat! This trip is terrible.

John: Terrible! It's tough sometimes, but it's the greatest adventure of our lives!

Elizabeth: Just think! We are off to a new land. Who knows what we could find!

Mary: Some wonderful things have happened on our voyage. Not long ago a baby was born on the *Mayflower*. His parents named him Oceanus, because he was born on the ocean.

Joseph: And during a storm, a man was thrown into the sea.

John: But he was saved! He grabbed onto a rope.

Elizabeth: See, our voyage has been pretty special. And all the trouble is worth it. In this new land, we'll have freedom to believe what we want to.

Sam: You guys are pretty brave!

John: Come on, everyone, let's go on deck.

[Everyone follows Elizabeth once around the Mayflower. Two sailors enter.]

Sailor #1: *[With arms folded across his chest.]* No children on deck! You'll only get in the way.

Sailor #2: Don't be so hard on them, mate. It's a nice day out.

Sailor #1: Not for long. Look at those clouds.

[Everyone stops and looks up at the sky.]

Sailor #2: Another storm is coming.

[Everyone begins to sway.]

Mary: Not another storm!

Joseph: *[Holding his stomach.]* I don't feel so good.

Sailor #1: Clear the deck!

Sailor #2: We'll be blown off course again.

[The storm is passing right over the ship. Everyone rocks with the ship with an "Ohhhh!" and an "Ahhh!" Finally the storm has passed. Everyone is so tired that they collapse in a heap on board. After a moment, Sam notices something off in the horizon.]

Sam: *[To himself.]* What's that? Is it land? It's land! *[To everyone.]* It's land!

Land! Everybody come look! It's land!

[Everyone gathers around Sam.]

All: It's land! We made it!

Sailor #1: Not so fast. It will be awhile before we can find a place to land.

Sam: If I remember my history, I think you'll find the perfect place on December 12. A place called Plymouth Rock.

John: Plymouth Rock. That's not a bad name.

All: Hooray! Hooray! Hooray for Plymouth Rock!

[The Pilgrims dance around Sam, jumping for joy. In the excitement, Sam leaves and climbs back into bed. The Pilgrims dance off stage.]

Act 3

Sam is sleeping in his bed. His parents enter.

Narrator: The next morning, Sam's mom and dad come into his bedroom. It's moving day.

Mom and Dad: Wake up, Sam. It's time for our adventure.

Sam: *[Jumps out of bed.]* All right!

[Mom and Dad look at each other.]

Mom: Sam, you sound a lot different than you did last night.

Dad: Last night you didn't want to move.

Sam: Well now I can't wait. If the Pilgrims could do it, so can I.

Mom and Dad: Whatever you say, Sam.

Sam: We're off to a new land. Who knows what we'll find there. Come on, let's go!

[Sam's parents smile and exit with their son.]

The End

Teacher's Guide

The Mayflower

Using the Play

This play can be performed with relatively few props, but for a larger production you may wish to construct one side of the *Mayflower* ship out of large pieces of cardboard. Actors can stand inside the *Mayflower* during Act 2.

The actors are required to pantomime many actions during the course of the play. Before introducing the play, you could lead students in a pantomime exercise as a warm-up by having them act out the different actions called for.

Background

The story of the *Mayflower* journey begins in England in the early 17th century, when English Puritans broke away from the Church of England. These people, called separatists, left England for Holland for 13 years before voting to move to America. To help finance the trip, they made a deal with a London merchant. When the ship left England on September 16, 1620, it carried about 102 passengers, less than half of whom were separatists, or Pilgrims. The other passengers were colonists looking to seek their fortune in the New World.

As the play describes, the conditions on the small, crowded ship were rough. In the only written record by a *Mayflower* passenger, William Bradford describes horrible seasickness, a leaky boat, and many fierce storms. Two people died on the long journey, but one boy was born at sea: Oceanus Hopkins.

After 65 days on the water, the ship sighted Cape Cod on November 19, 1620. The passengers searched for a suitable place to settle for weeks until they finally landed at Plymouth, Massachusetts, on December 26, 1620.

Book Links

Across the Wide Dark Sea: The Mayflower Journey by Jean Van Leeuwen, pictures by Thomas B. Allen (Dial Books for Young Readers, 1995)

The First Thanksgiving Feast by Joan Anderson, photographs by George Ancona (Clarion Books, 1989)

If You Sailed on the Mayflower in 1620 by Ann McGovern (Scholastic, 1991)

On the Mayflower: Voyage of a Ship Apprentice and a Passenger Girl by Kate Waters, photographs by Russ Kendall (Scholastic, 1996)

Extending the Play

On the Move

After reading the play, discuss the story. Ask: *Why do you think Sam was afraid to move?* (Answers may include: He didn't want to leave his house and his friends; sometimes things we don't know about can be scary to us.) *Where did Sam go in his dream?* (He went back in time on the *Mayflower*.) *What was it like for the kids on the* Mayflower? (It was crowded; there were storms; they had to eat hard bread as well as cheese, beans, and salted pork; there was nothing to do because the kids had to leave their toys at home.) *Why do you think*

Sam felt better about moving after his dream? (Because he was inspired by the Pilgrims' bravery and sense of hope for the future.)

To help students compare and contrast Sam's move with the Pilgrims' move, you can make a two-column chart. Ask children to imagine that they were moving from England to the United States today. How would their move differ from the move years ago? Your chart may look something like this:

Moving Today	The Pilgrims' Move
airplane	boat
6 hours	65 days
a hot meal	hardtack
can bring all your toys	had to leave toys at home
can learn about the U.S. on the Internet or in the library	didn't know a lot about their new home

If any of your students remember making a move, ask them to share their experiences with the class.

Mayflower Journey

Ask students to imagine that they are a passenger on the *Mayflower* and to write about their experiences on the ship. Books such as *Across the Wide Dark Sea* and *On the Mayflower* will provide kids with more factual information on which to base their accounts.

Encourage students to answer these questions in their accounts:
What does the ship look like?
What do you do during the day?
What do you eat?
How does it feel to be caught in a storm?
How do you feel about the move?

A Snowman for Mrs. McKay

by Jane Manners

Characters

* Narrator (teacher or older child)
* Mrs. McKay
* Child 1
* Child 2
* Child 3
* Child 4
* Child 5
* Child 6
  (More children may be used if desired.)

Props

* white confetti "snow"
* posterboard "snowman"

Act 1

Mrs. McKay sits in a chair onstage. The narrator enters and begins the story.

Narrator: Once upon a wintertime, there lived a nice, elderly woman named Mrs. McKay. *[Mrs. McKay waves to the audience.]* Mrs. McKay loved to look out her window and watch all of the busy children go by.

[The children enter, one or two at a time. They wave to Mrs. McKay and then walk to the other side of the stage.]

Narrator: The children always said hello to Mrs. McKay. And Mrs. McKay always had a smile for them. One day, the children began to worry that Mrs. McKay would be alone for the holidays. The children called out:

Children: Oh, Mrs. McKay! Oh, Mrs. McKay!
　　　　　How will you spend the holiday?

Narrator: And Mrs. McKay said:

Mrs. McKay: Don't worry about me!

Narrator: As the children huddled together to stay warm, they noticed something in the air.

[The children throw white confetti in the air.]

Children: It's snowing! It's snowing!

Narrator: The snow gave the children a wonderful idea.

Children: Let's make a snowman!
Let's make it today!
Let's make a snowman
for Mrs. McKay!

Child 1: Now she won't be alone for the holiday!

Act 2

Mrs. McKay leaves the stage. The other children are gathered next to her "house." As each child steps forward to describe the action, the others should act it out.

Child 1: Take some snow,
start out small,
pat, pat, pat,
it's a ball.

Child 2: Take the ball,
nice and round,
roll, roll, roll,
on the ground.

Child 3: Make one more,
start out small,
pat, pat, pat,
it's a ball.

Child 4: Take the ball,
         nice and round,
         roll, roll, roll,
         on the ground.

Child 5: Make one more,
         start out small,
         pat, pat, pat,
         it's a ball.

Child 6: Take the ball,
         nice and round,
         roll, roll, roll,
         on the ground.

[Two children bring the snowman out onstage.]

Children: Now we have it!
         One, two, three.
         It's a snowman!
         Look and see!

Act 3

Mrs. McKay has returned to her chair.

Narrator: The children made a wonderful snowman for Mrs. McKay. They

couldn't wait to show her. So they all went over to Mrs. McKay's house and knocked on her door.

Children: Knock, knock, knock.

Narrator: When the door opened, the children took Mrs. McKay by the hand and led her to the snowman.

Mrs. McKay: What a wonderful present!

Narrator: The children had made Mrs. McKay very happy. Now when Mrs. McKay looked out her window, she would see the smiling face of the snowman.

[Mrs. McKay and the children dance in a circle around the snowman.]

Children: We made a snowman!
We made it today!
We made a snowman
for Mrs. McKay!

All: Hip, hip, hooray!

The End

Teacher's Guide

A Snowman for Mrs. McKay

Using the Play

While this play can be performed by students of all ages, it was especially written with young students in mind. In the role of narrator, the teacher is in the ideal position to direct the action of the children. The children's rhyming lines can be written out separately and given to the actors to memorize at home.

We've suggested using white confetti to represent snow, but if you don't want a blizzard in your classroom, you may wish to have some children pantomime the falling snow.

Background

You may wish to perform this play during the winter holiday season. Many cultures celebrate major holidays near the first day of winter, which falls between December 20 to 22, and is the one day of the year when the night is at its longest. After this day, the days get longer and longer. The focus of many winter holidays is community, family, and a sense of hope for the year to come. Christmas, Hanukkah, Kwanzaa, and Ramadan are just some of the holidays that your students may celebrate at this time of year.

This play can also be used when you're studying snow with your students. Snow is formed of tiny crystals of frozen water. These crystals cluster together to form snowflakes as they fall through Earth's atmosphere. Snow crystals can only form in temperatures below freezing, or 32 degrees Fahrenheit, so children living in areas where the temperature does not freeze may not get to see snow often, if at all.

Book Links

The Adventure of the Big Snow by Nancy McArthur (Little Apple, 1998)

The Biggest, Best Snowman by Margaret Cuyler (Scholastic, 1998)

The Snowy Day by Ezra Jack Keats (Puffin Books, 1976)

Extending the Play

Helping Hands

After you read the play for the first time, discuss the story. Ask: *Why were the children concerned about Mrs. McKay?* (They didn't want her to be alone on the holiday.) *Why did the children make the snowman?* (To cheer up Mrs. McKay; to show Mrs. McKay that she wasn't alone.) *Did Mrs. McKay like the snowman? How can you tell?* (She was happy when she saw the snowman, and she danced with the children.)

Lead students in a discussion about helping others. Have they ever done something nice for somebody else? How did it make them feel? How do they feel when somebody does something nice for them?

Invite students to trace one of their hands on a piece of construction paper, and then cut out the outline of the hand. Call these "helping hands" and ask children to think of one way that people can help one another and write it on the hand. Display the helping hands on a wall or bulletin board.

Making Snowpeople

As a class, read the book *Snowballs* by Lois Ehlert (Harcourt Brace and Company, 1995). In the book, the young narrator describes how her family saves "good stuff" to put on the snow people they make. This "good stuff" includes everything from pasta shells to colorful scarves and hats.

After reading the book, invite children to bring in "good stuff" from home to make their own snow people. You may wish to send a note home to parents, informing them that they should include any scraps that they wouldn't mind being used in a collage, such as old buttons, ribbons, bows, old greeting cards, scraps of colorful tissue paper or wrapping paper, etc. Then have children use their "good stuff" to make paper snow people, using white cardboard circles or paper plates for a base. Use the pictures in *Snowballs* for inspiration.

Weather Watch

Before your winter season begins, ask students to predict how many inches of snow you will receive this year.

Draw a large bar graph on a piece of posterboard. The simple graph can be a vertical bar, with marks up the side representing inches. Post the graph in your classroom and as winter progresses, keep track of how much snow has fallen by filling in the bar graph. After the last snowfall, compare your graph to the prediction you made earlier in the year. How close was your guess?

The Rabbit Who Stole Groundhog Day

by Tracey West

Characters

* Narrator
* Carterville Cal
* Mrs. Groundhog
* Mr. Groundhog
* Kenneth Rabbit
* Molly Mole
* Reporter #1
* Reporter #2

Props

* a sign reading: "This way to Cal's Famous Groundhog Hole"
* a large cardboard arrow

Act 1

Narrator: In a snug burrow under the ground, a groundhog named Carterville Cal was hibernating peacefully.

Mrs. Groundhog: Cal, wake up!

Mr. Groundhog: Your big day is almost here.

Cal: *[Sleepily.]* What? Is it time to get up already?

Mrs. Groundhog: You know that you have to get up early every year. The whole world is waiting for you. Tomorrow is February 2.

Mr. Groundhog: That's right! They all want to know if Carterville Cal will see his shadow on Groundhog Day.

Mrs. Groundhog: If it's sunny and you see your shadow, that means there will be six more weeks of winter. But if it is cloudy and you can't see your shadow, spring will come early.

Cal: *[Stretching and yawning.]* Humans are so silly sometimes! That's just an old story. Why do they think that I can predict the weather? I'm a groundhog, not a meteorologist.

Mr. Groundhog: A meaty what?

Cal: A meteorologist. A scientist who studies the weather. They use machines to study the water and the air and the wind. They can tell if the rest of the

winter will be cold and snowy, or if it will be warm, like spring.

Mrs. Groundhog: But Cal, it's a tradition. People are counting on you!

Cal: Why don't they just watch my cousin, Punxsutawney Phil, in Pennsylvania? He's famous.

Mrs. Groundhog: That's true, Cal. But Pennsylvania is so far away from Carterville. This is your hometown.

Mr. Groundhog: You can't let the people of Carterville down!

Cal: *[Climbs out of bed.]* Oh, all right. I'll do it. But I still think it's silly!

Narrator: Kenneth Rabbit, Cal's neighbor, was listening to Cal and his parents through a wall in the burrow.

Kenneth: *[To audience.]* Carterville Cal is famous! I wish I could be like him. *[Kenneth thinks.]* Hmmm. Maybe I can. I think I know a way.

Act 2

* Scene 1 *

Narrator: That night, Kenneth Rabbit crawled through the tunnels of the groundhog burrow. He found the sign that pointed to Cal's famous groundhog hole.

Kenneth: This is so easy! All I have to do is move this arrow. Cal will get lost. Everyone will be waiting for him to pop out of his hole. But instead of Cal, I will pop out! I will be a hero.

Narrator: Just then, Molly Mole crawled by.

Molly: Kenneth! I may not be able to see very well, but I can tell you're up to no good. What are you doing?

Kenneth: N-n-nothing, Molly.

Molly: Kenneth, tell me the truth.

Kenneth: *[Hangs head.]* OK Molly. I was just trying to confuse Cal so he couldn't pop out of his hole tomorrow.

Molly: *[Shocked.]* Why would you want to do that?

Kenneth: Cal always gets all of the attention! I thought I could pop out of the hole instead of him. Besides, he doesn't want to do it anyway.

Molly: We'll see about that!

* Scene 2 *

Narrator: Molly went to find Cal as fast as she could.

Molly: Cal! Cal! You won't believe what just happened.

Narrator: Molly told Kenneth the whole story.

Molly: He wants to pop out of the hole instead of you! Whoever heard of a rabbit popping out of a hole on Groundhog Day?

Cal: *[Thinking.]* Hmm. That's an interesting idea.

Act 3

* Scene 1 *

Narrator: The next morning, Mr. and Mrs. Groundhog ran into Cal's room before the sun came up.

Mrs. Groundhog: Wake up, Cal! Wake up!

Mr. Groundhog: Today's the day!

Cal: *[Coughing.]* I don't feel so well.

Mrs. Groundhog: Oh no!

Mr. Groundhog: What will we do?

Cal: We'll have to find someone else to pop out of the hole.

Mrs. Groundhog: But who?

Mr. Groundhog: I could do it. But my name is Reginald. "Carterville Reginald" just doesn't sound right.

Mrs. Groundhog: Neither does "Carterville Ethel."

Molly: *[Walks in.]* I guess that leaves me out, too.

Cal: We need someone with the perfect name. If only Kenneth Rabbit were here.

Narrator: Kenneth Rabbit was listening again, and he hopped right in.

Kenneth: Kenneth Rabbit, at your service.

Cal: Kenneth, you've got to pop out of the hole for me today. You can be Carterville Ken. It's perfect.

Mrs. Groundhog: Whoever heard of a rabbit popping out of a hole on Groundhog Day?

Cal: Those silly humans won't care. They'll probably like it.

Kenneth: I don't know what to say, Cal. It's my dream come true. Thank you.

Cal: You're welcome, Kenneth. Now you'd better get moving. The sun's almost up!

Narrator: Kenneth hopped out of Cal's room.

Cal: [*Jumps out of bed.*] Come on! Let's go see Kenneth in action!

Mrs. Groundhog: Cal! I thought you were sick.

Cal: Sorry, Mom. I wasn't sick. I was just tired of those silly humans. Besides, I wanted to do something nice for Kenneth.

* Scene 2 *

Narrator: Outside Cal's famous groundhog hole, reporters from all over the world were gathered.

Reporter #1: The sun is almost up. Carterville Cal will be popping up any minute now.

Reporter #2: Will spring arrive early? Or will we get six more weeks of winter?

Kenneth: [*Pops out of hole.*] What a cloudy day! I think I'll hop around for a little bit. I guess that means spring will come early, everyone!

Reporter #1: A rabbit? Whoever heard of a rabbit popping out of a hole on Groundhog Day?

Reporter #2: Are you kidding? This is amazing! What a story!

Reporter #1: Mr. Rabbit, the world wants to know who you are!

Kenneth: Carterville Ken, at your service!

[The reporters surround Kenneth, asking him questions and taking his picture.]

Kenneth: I'd like to thank my good friend Carterville Cal for making this possible!

Narrator: Cal and his parents were watching from nearby.

Mrs. Groundhog: Cal, aren't you going to miss all of this?

Cal: No way, Mom. It's way too silly for me. I can prove it, too.

Mr. Groundhog: How, Cal?

Cal: I watched the weather report this morning. There's going to be a blizzard tomorrow!

The End

Teacher's Guide

The Rabbit Who Stole Groundhog Day

Using the Play

When staging this play, you may want to divide the stage area into three sections: stage left for Cal's room, center stage for the area of tunnels with the sign and the arrow, and stage right for Cal's famous groundhog hole.

Background

On the morning of February 2, people in North America anxiously wait to find out if a groundhog emerging from its hole that morning scurried back into its hole after seeing its shadow. Legend says that if the day is sunny and the groundhog sees its shadow, there will be six more weeks of winter. If the day is cloudy, however, that signals an early spring.

Europeans have a similar tradition, and in fact, many believe this is where the legend began. February 2 occurs about six weeks before the official first day of spring. It is also a Christian holiday called Candlemas Day. In some countries, it was also the first day of spring planting. According to an old English song:

If Candlemas be fair and bright,
Come, winter, have another flight.
If Candlemas brings clouds and rain,
Go, winter, and come not again.

The English used a badger or a hedgehog to predict the weather, but that animal was replaced by the groundhog (also known as a woodchuck) in the New World. The groundhog is a member of the squirrel family that lives underground in elaborate burrows. They hibernate during the winter and usually emerge around the second week of February.

While Carterville Cal is a fictional groundhog, there is a groundhog named Punxsutawney Phil. He's televised every

Groundhog Day emerging from his hole in Pennsylvania.

Book Links

Geoffrey Groundhog Predicts the Weather by Bruce Koscielniak (Houghton Mifflin Co., 1995)

Gretchen Groundhog, It's Your Day! by Abby Levine (Albert Whitman and Co., 1998)

It's Groundhog Day! by Steve Kroll (Scholastic Trade, 1995)

Extending the Play

Testing the Legend

On February 2, watch the news report on the most famous groundhog in the U.S., Punxsutawney Phil of Pennsylvania. Does Phil see his shadow? Make a note of Phil's prediction.

Over the next six weeks, keep track of the weather on a chart. What is the temperature each day? Does it rain? Does it snow? After six weeks, study the chart. Did springlike weather arrive early? If you are still experiencing winter weather, keep updating your chart until spring weather arrives. Compare the results of your record-keeping with Phil's prediction. Would the groundhog make a good meteorologist? Why or why not?

Amazing Alliterations

Cal chooses Kenneth Rabbit as his replacement for a few reasons: He doesn't want to be a celebrity groundhog anymore; he feels sorry for Kenneth; and he likes the way "Carterville Ken" sounds. Use this nickname as a springboard to explore alliteration with your students. In alliteration, the same initial sound is repeated in two or more words. Alliteration is a fun way to explore consonant and vowel sounds, especially those sounds that can be created by different letters, for example, *c* and *k*, *c* and *s*, *f* and *ph*, *g* and *j*, etc.

Here are some ways to explore alliteration with your students:

* Have students make up an alliterative nickname for themselves, such as Powerful Pam and Terrific Tony.

* Challenge students to make alliterative sentences, such as "Silly snakes sleep silently." How many words can they use in their sentences? See whose sentence is the longest.

* Create picture word cards using drawings, stickers, or pictures cut out from magazines, and have students sort the cards according to their initial sound.

Cupid's Day Off

by Katherine Noll

Characters

* Julia
* Laurie
* Robby
* Mrs. Jordan
* Newscaster
* England Reporter
* Emily
* Denmark Reporter
* Italy Reporter
* Cupid

Props

* Valentine's Day decorations
* a box
* a backpack
* a valentine

Act 1

A classroom. The lights are dim, and children are just entering the room

Julia: I'm so happy! It's almost time for the Valentine's Day party. I filled out all my cards last night.

Robby: My Mom made cupcakes with pink icing. I can't wait to eat them.

[Mrs. Jordan enters the room and turns on the lights. The room is bare of any decorations.]

Julia: *[Looking around in surprise.]* Mrs. Jordan, where are all the decorations? What happened to them?

Mrs. Jordan: You didn't hear the news yet? Oh dear, it's terrible.

Laurie: What news?

Mrs. Jordan: There isn't going to be a Valentine's Day this year.

Robby: What? But there has to be a Valentine's Day! My Mom made cupcakes. See? *[He lifts the foil off the box he was carrying and holds up the box.]* Look! *[He looks into the box.]* Oh no! The cupcakes have disappeared. And I was so hungry!

Julia: I have all my valentines right here. *[She reaches into her backpack and pulls out a bag.]* The bag is empty! Where did everything go?

Act 2

Mrs. Jordan: Children, let's settle down. I'm going to turn on the news so we can find out exactly what is going on.

[Mrs. Jordan walks over to the TV set and turns it on.]

Newscaster: Good morning everyone. Our top news story is that there will be no Valentine's Day today. Valentine's Day is held every year on February 14. It is a day that honors love and friendship. But this year, something is wrong. Valentine cards, flowers, and chocolates are vanishing all over the world. Here is our reporter in England with the reaction over there.

England Reporter: I am standing here with Miss Emily Carnegie. Emily, what do you think about Valentine's Day?

Emily: I'm very upset. Here in England we sing special Valentine songs. My Mum made her special Valentine buns with caraway seeds. The buns are gone. And no one can remember the songs!

England Reporter: How awful! Now to our reporter in Denmark.

Denmark Reporter: Here in Denmark people are very upset. It is the tradition here for people to send pressed white flowers called snowdrops to their friends. Every white flower in the country has disappeared. Let's hear what's happening in Italy.

Italian Reporter: Here in Italy there were many feasts planned for

Valentine's Day. They have all been canceled!

Newscaster: This just in! Cupid has been found! That's right, Cupid, the cherub who is in charge of Valentine's Day. He is here in this studio.

[Cupid enters, looking angry.]

Newscaster: Cupid, what is going on? The entire world wants to know—what's happened to Valentine's Day?

Cupid: What's happened to Valentine's Day? I'll tell you what's happened to Valentine's Day! I canceled it.

Newscaster: But Cupid, why?

Cupid: Every year I work hard to get ready for Valentine's Day. The decorations, the chocolates, not to mention flying around and spreading love throughout the world. And do you think I have ever gotten a box of chocolates? some flowers? one crummy valentine? Nope, not ever. No one has ever sent me anything.

Newscaster: That's a shame, Cupid, but surely you can't ruin everyone's Valentine's Day because of it?

Cupid: Just watch me!

[Cupid storms out of the newsroom. The Newscaster shakes her head. Mrs. Jordan walks over to the TV and turns it off.]

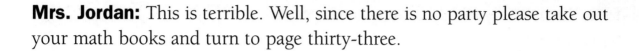

Mrs. Jordan: This is terrible. Well, since there is no party please take out your math books and turn to page thirty-three.

Julia: Mrs. Jordan, we can't just sit here and do math while Valentine's Day is ruined! We've got to do something!

Robby: Yeah, I'm hungry. I want my cupcakes back.

Laurie: I have an idea. Maybe if we invite Cupid to our party, he won't be so angry.

Robby: There is no party.

Julia: Let's have one anyway.

Mrs. Jordan: I'll send an invitation by special delivery to Cupid right away.

Act 3

The classroom is decorated for Valentine's Day. The children are sitting down.

All: The decorations are back!

Robby: *[Looking into his box.]* So are my cupcakes!

Julia: *[Looking into her backpack.]* So are my valentines!

Mrs. Jordan: It looks like Cupid changed his mind about Valentine's Day. Now we can have our party.

[Cupid enters.]

All: It's Cupid!

Cupid: Hi, everyone. I just want to say how sorry I am.

Laurie: That's okay, Cupid.

Cupid: *[Shakes head.]* You were nice to me, even though I wasn't so nice to you. I shouldn't have tried to ruin everyone's Valentine's Day just because I was angry. I should have talked about how I was feeling instead.

Mrs. Jordan: We're glad you accepted our invitation. And you made up for what you did by giving us back Valentine's Day!

[Laurie walks up to Cupid. She is holding a large valentine.]

Laurie: Here, Cupid. This is for you. *[She hands Cupid the valentine.]*

Cupid: A valentine for me! Nobody has ever given me one before.

[Cupid opens the Valentine and reads it.]

"Dear Cupid,
We are sorry we always forget you on Valentine's Day.
We promise to send you a valentine every year.

Have a great Valentine's Day!
Your friends in Mrs. Jordan's Class"

Cupid: How nice! Thank you all so much! I promise never to ruin Valentine's Day again. Now, let's have a party!

Robby: Finally, I get to eat!

All: Happy Valentine's Day!

The End

Teacher's Guide

Cupid's Day Off

Using the Play

When staging the play, your prop crew will need to be aware of when the Valentine's Day decorations, cupcakes, and cards "reappear" and come up with a plan to make this happen smoothly between Act 2 and Act 3.

In Act 2, a fun way to stage the television scenes might be to take a large box and cut a square out of one side, then decorate it to look like a TV set. The newscaster and news reporters can step behind the box when it is their turn to say their lines.

Background

How did Valentine's Day begin? There are many possibilities. Legend says that in the third century, a Christian priest was martyred on February 14, when he was killed for performing marriages against the will of the Emperor Claudius II.

However the holiday started, the modern holiday as we know it became popular during Victorian times. Victorians took advantage of new printing technology and began sending one another elaborate cards with flowers, hearts, doves, and cupids. Usually depicted as a winged cherub holding a bow and arrow, Cupid originated as the son of Venus, the Roman goddess of love. Legend says that if Cupid shoots his arrow into your heart, you will fall in love.

Book Links

Arthur's Valentine by Marc Brown (Little, Brown, and Company, 1998)

One Very Best Valentine's Day by Joan W. Blos, illustrated by Emily Arnold McCully (Aladdin Paperbacks, 1990)

Silly Tilly's Valentine by Lillian Hoban (HarperCollins, 1998)

Extending the Play

Valentine Rhymes

Everyone knows this popular valentine rhyme:

Roses are red,
Violets are blue,
Sugar is sweet,
And so are you.

Write this rhyme on the chalkboard and ask students to identify the rhyming words. Then invite students to make up their own valentine rhymes, using the following rhyme starters, or one of your own:

Roses are red,
lizards are green . . .

Roses are red,
bubblegum is pink . . .

Roses are red,
daisies are yellow . . .

The sun is hot,
The ice is cold . . .

Lemons are sour,
Sugar is sweet . . .

Valentine's Day Around the World

In the story, students learn about Valentine's Day customs in different countries. After reading the play, see if children can locate England, Denmark, and Italy on a map of the world. Then discuss the customs. How are they similar to U.S. Valentine's Day customs? How are they different?

Mail Bag Math

Students enjoy making bags to hold the valentines they will receive in class. You can combine this classic activity and add a math twist.

For each mail bag, you will need a paper lunch bag. Have students cut out the following shapes to put on their bags: red hearts, pink hearts, white hearts, and red flowers. Put the shapes in a common area and instruct students to decorate their bags by attaching the shapes with paste, using as many or as few shapes as they want.

When students have finished their bags, they can create simple quantity graphs to show how many shapes they used. To make the graphs, instruct students to divide a sheet of paper into four parts. In one part write "Red Hearts," then "Pink Hearts," then "White Hearts," then "Red Flowers." In each section, students should draw the number of shapes they used on their bags. When the graphs are finished, ask: *Which shape did you use the most? Which shape did you use the least? How can you tell by looking at the graph?*

Students can tape the finished bags to their desks and use them to receive cards.

April Fools the School

by Tracey West

Characters

* April
* Dad
* Mom
* Mr. Fine
* Sarah
* Brendan
* Evan
* Linda
* Misty
* Student #1
* Student #2
* Additional Students

Props

* classroom desks
* paper lunch bag
* fake snake (rubber or paper)
* clock with movable hands

Act 1

* Scene 1 *

April's kitchen. April is eating breakfast with her parents.

Dad: Tomorrow's your big day, April!

April: Dad, you know I hate April Fool's Day! Just because my name is April Poole, everyone calls me April Fool. They play tricks on me all day.

Mom: It's all in fun, April.

Dad: I think it's cool, April Fool!

April: *[Rolls her eyes.]* Dad! It's not funny.

Mom: Maybe it would be more fun if you got into the April Fool's Day spirit.

Dad: Sure. You could fool the kids in school.

April: Hmmm. I never thought of that before. But how could I do that?

Mom: *[Looks out the window.]* April, your bus is coming.

April: *[Jumps up from the table.]* See you later!

* Scene 2 *

April's classroom. The students are talking in small groups before the bell rings.

Sarah: *[Approaches April.]* Hi, April. What's the matter? You look worried.

April: Hi, Sarah. *[Whispers.]* You know. Tomorrow's April Fool's Day. That's the worst day of the year.

Brendan: *[Runs up to the girls, followed by Evan.]* Hey look! It's the April Fool!

Evan: I can't wait until tomorrow, April Fool.

April: That's not funny, you guys.

Linda: *[Walks up with Misty.]* What's the matter, April? Can't you take a joke?

Misty: Yeah, can't you take a joke?

[The bell rings. Mr. Fine walks into the classroom.]

Mr. Fine: Settle down, class. What's everyone so excited about?

Linda: Tomorrow is April Fool's Day, Mr. Fine.

Mr. Fine: That's right! I can see why you're excited. April Fool's Day is one of my favorite days of the year.

April: *[Raises hand.]* Uh, Mr. Fine, isn't playing tricks on April Fool's Day against the rules or something?

Mr. Fine: Well, there are some rules. April Fool's Day pranks should never be mean. And they should never hurt anybody. But if they're clever and fun, then I think they're OK. Who knows? I may even have a trick or two up my sleeve.

Brendan: I've got lots of tricks, Mr. Fine. *[Turns and looks at April, and whispers.]* And they're all for you!

Linda: *[Looks at April.]* I can't wait until tomorrow, Mr. Fine.

Misty: *[Looks at April.]* Yeah, I can't wait until tomorrow.

[April looks worried. Then she gets a smile on her face. She raises her hand.]

Mr. Fine: Yes, April?

April: I can't wait until tomorrow either, Mr. Fine. I think you will all be in for a surprise. This year, I am planning the biggest April Fool's Day trick ever!

[The class reacts in surprise.]

Sarah: *[Whispers to April.]* April, what are you going to do?

April: It's the best idea ever. *[She leans over and whispers in Sarah's ear.]*

Act 2

* Scene 1 *

April Fool's Day. The students talk in small groups before the bell rings. Sarah enters, wearing a raincoat.

Brendan: Hey, Sarah, where's your friend the April Fool?

Linda: And why are you wearing a raincoat? It's sunny out today.

Misty: Yeah, it's sunny today.

Sarah: April should be here any minute. She's busy planning her April Fool's Day trick.

Evan: I don't believe it. April's never played a trick on anybody.

Linda: What is she planning to do, anyway?

Sarah: I can't say. But I'm sure glad I wore this raincoat.

Brendan: She must be planning something huge! Come on, you've got to tell us what it is!

Sarah: *[Looks around to make sure no one else is listening.]* OK. I can tell you this. April will play her trick at exactly 2:30 P.M.

[The bell rings. April enters, and Mr. Fine is right behind her.]

Mr. Fine: OK, class, please take your seats and take out your pencils. It's

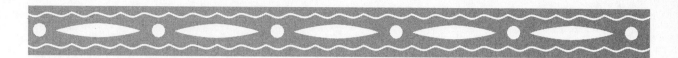

time for the big math test.

[Students react in surprise.]

Evan: Math test? What math test?

Linda: You didn't tell us there was going to be a math test.

Misty: No, you didn't tell us.

Mr. Fine: Got you! Happy April Fool's Day!

Brendan: That was a good one, Mr. Fine.

Mr. Fine: I'd still like you to take out your math books, please. There's no test, but we still have a math lesson today.

[The students go to open their desks. April tries to open hers, but can't—her desk has been turned backwards. The class giggles.]

Linda: April Fool, April!

April: *[Smiles calmly.]* Is that your April Fool's Day trick, Linda? That's nothing compared to my big trick.

Evan: *[To Brendan.]* She didn't care about that trick at all. She really must be planning something big!

✴ Scene 2 ✴

The lunch room. Students are sitting around tables and talking. April is holding a

paper lunch bag.

Student #1: I hear she's planning something big!

Student #2: Brendan said it was going to happen at 2:30.

Brendan: That's what she thinks. But she won't have the guts after she sees my trick.

[April opens her lunch bag. She pulls out a fake snake.]

April: *[Not scared at all.]* Mmm. Mmm. This looks delicious.

Evan: She didn't even scream!

Brendan: Maybe she *is* planning something big after all.

* Scene 3 *

Back in Mr. Fine's classroom. The clock reads 2:29. The students are nervously looking at the clock.

Mr. Fine: Class, is something wrong? You look strange.

Brendan: Everything's fine, Mr. Fine.

Evan: Sure. It's not like we're worried about a big April Fool's trick or anything.

Linda: Yes we are, Mr. Fine. It's April. She's planning a really big trick.

Misty: Yeah, a really big trick!

Brendan: Oh no! It's 2:30! Everybody watch out!

[All of the students duck under their desks or cover their heads, except Sarah and April. After a few seconds, they slowly look around.]

Evan: Hey! Nothing happened.

Linda: April didn't trick us after all.

Sarah: Oh, yes she did!

April: I sure did! I had you all believing that I was going to do the biggest trick ever. I fooled you all. You looked pretty funny hiding under your desks.

Mr. Fine: That was pretty clever, April. *[To the class.]* I guess April was finally repaying you for playing tricks on her all these years.

Brendan: I guess you're right. Sorry, April.

Linda: I have to admit that was a pretty good trick.

Misty: Yeah, a pretty good trick.

April: I guess that's why they call me April Fool!

The End

Teacher's Guide

April Fools the School

Using the Play

To help build suspense at the end of the play, use paper fasteners to create a clock with movable hands and large numbers. Recruit a student to turn the big hand to 2:30 right after the line, "Yeah, a really big trick!"

Background

"The first of April, some do say, is set apart for All Fool's Day. But why people call it so, nor I, nor themselves do know. But on this day are people set on purpose of pure merriment."

Ben Franklin pondered the origins of April Fool's Day in *Poor Robin's Almanac* in 1790. Although this day is celebrated all over the world (but not always on April 1), it is difficult to pin down where or why it started. What we do know is that the custom was probably brought to the colonies by English, Scottish, and French settlers and has remained popular throughout the centuries.

Book Links

Arthur's April Fool by Marc Brown (Little, Brown and Company, 1985)

Elmer Again by David McKee (Lothrop, Lee and Shepard, 1992)

Look Out, It's April Fool's Day by Frank Modell (Greenwillow, 1985)

Mud Flat April Fool by James Stevenson (Greenwillow, 1998)

Extending the Play

The Spirit of April Fool's Day

After reading the play, discuss the story. Do students think April's trick was a good one? What do they think about the students who play tricks on April every year?

Remind students of Mr. Fine's rules that April Fool's Day tricks should not be mean, or hurt anyone. What do students think of these rules? What other rules can they make up for April Fool's Day?

Ask students to share their April Fool's Day experiences. Did they ever play a trick on someone? Did they ever have a trick played on them? Was it fun? How did they feel?

Sound Sorting

Ask students to find the two words in the play's title that rhyme: *fool* and *school*. Introduce the long /oo/ sound. Can student find other words in the play with this sound? (*cool*, *rules*, *Poole*)

You can review the long /oo/ sound and the short /oo/ sound with a folder sorting activity. In the left-hand side of the folder, create one large pocket to hold word cards. In the right-hand side of the folder, create two pockets: a yellow pocket labeled "oo as in fool," and a blue pocket labeled "oo as in good." On small index cards, write the following words: *boot, cool, hoop, moon, pool, school, soon, too, book, cook, foot, hood, hook, look, stood, took,* and *wood*.

An instruction sheet in the front of the folder should read: "Sort the word cards. Put each word into the correct pocket." To make this a self-checking activity, put a yellow dot on the back of the long /oo/ word cards, and a blue dot on the back of the short /oo/ word cards.

Invent a Holiday

April Poole feels like April Fool's Day is a holiday just for her. Ask students to imagine that they can invent a holiday of their own. What special thing would the day celebrate? What name would they give it? What kind of food would people eat on that day? Invite students to make a poster or write a paragraph describing their holiday. To take it further, ask students to vote on the proposed holidays, and celebrate the winning idea as a class. Have a holiday party, make holiday cards, and write holiday songs to celebrate your own special day.

Spreading the Sun

a Cherokee myth

adapted by Paula Thomas

Characters

* Narrator
* Rat
* Sheep
* Wolf
* Moose
* Coyote
* Possum
* Buzzard
* Deer
* Grandmother Spider

Props

* yellow cardboard sun
* yellow helium balloon
* piece of clay
* "clay" pot or bowl

Act 1

The stage is divided into two parts. One part is the dark side of the world and the other is the light side of the world.

Narrator: The people of the Cherokee Nation believe that the world was not always as it is today. They tell of a time when the earth was divided. One half was always dark and the other was always light. Life was not always easy for those living in darkness. *[Points to the darkened half of the stage.]* Look over there, and you'll see what I mean.

[The animals on the dark half of the world start to move around, bumping into each other as they go.]

Rat: *[To Sheep.]* Hey, watch where you're going! You nearly stepped on me.

Sheep: It wasn't my fault. Moose bumped into me!

Moose: Hey don't blame me! I was just trying to get out of the water. I fell into a pond back there!

Sheep: I wish that we could see in the dark like wolf does. He never gets stepped on!

Moose: Or goes swimming when he doesn't want to!

Wolf: Things would be a lot better for everyone if you could see where you

were going, like I can. I think that I have an idea!

[All of the animals gather around Wolf.]

Wolf: What we really need is some light around here. We should go to the other side of the world and ask for a small piece of their sun. I'm sure that they will share!

Coyote: *[Sneering.]* Share? No way! Don't you think they would have already given us some sun if they were willing to share? If we want a piece of their sun we are going to have to steal it!

[All of the animals nod in agreement.]

Wolf: We can't steal a piece! Stealing is wrong!

Coyote: Don't worry, Wolf. We are only going to take a really little piece. They won't even know that it's gone. *[To the group.]* Does everyone agree with the plan?

All: Let's do it!

Sheep: Who is going to go? And how are they going to get there?

Possum: Let me! I can do it!

Wolf: Who is that?

Possum: *[Shyly.]* Please let me try. I've got these really long claws that I use

for digging. I can dig a tunnel to the other side.

Sheep: How will you get the sun back?

Possum: I'll just hide it in my tail! It's so big and bushy no one will see it there!

Wolf: OK, Brave Possum. Go, but be careful!

Possum: I'll start right now! *[Walks to the divider between the worlds and begins digging.]*

All: Good luck!.

Act 2

Possum: *[Crawls out from the divider onto the light side of the world.]* Oh, my! *[shielding his eyes from the sun.]* That sun is so bright it's hurting my eyes! But a possum's got to do what a possum's got to do!

[Possum runs to the sun, takes a piece, and hides it in his tail. He then runs and climbs back under the divider to the dark side.]

Wolf: Look, it's Possum! He's on fire! Quick, get water!

[Sheep and Moose run to Possum and throw water on his tail.]

Moose: [*Pointing at Possum's tail.*] Look Possum, your tail is skinny. All the fur is *gone!*

Sheep: And the light is gone, too! When we put out the fire we put out the sun.

Wolf: What are we going to do now?

Buzzard: I am just the right bird for the job.

Coyote: Why do you think you can do it?

Buzzard: Look at my super crown of feathers. It's just the place for hiding a piece of the sun. I'll fly down the tunnel that Possum dug. I'll be back in a jiffy!

Wolf: OK, but be careful!

All: Good luck!

[*Buzzard waves and flies to the tunnel.*]

Act 3

Buzzard: [*Flies out from the divider onto the light side of the world.*] If I hurry no one will even notice me! [*He flies to the sun, takes a piece, and hides it in his crown. He then goes back under the divider to the dark side.*]

Deer: Look, everyone! Buzzard is back!

Buzzard: Ow! My head! It's on fire! Ow, ow, owww!

[Deer and Coyote run and throw water on Buzzard's head.]

Deer: Buzzard, your head! Your crown is gone. You are bald!

Buzzard: What about the sun? Where is the sun I brought back?

Wolf: I'm afraid it's the same as the last time. It was put out by the water.

Deer: What are we going to do now?

Grandmother Spider: I can go! I can do it.

Coyote: No way, Grandmother Spider. I don't want to be rude but you are way too old and way too slow.

Grandmother Spider: I may be old and slow, but I know that I am the one for this job. All I need is a piece of clay.

Deer: *[Goes to a table and returns with a piece of clay.]* Here is the clay, Grandmother Spider. What are you going to do with it?

Grandmother Spider: Watch. *[She leans over and shapes the clay into a pot.]* See! *[She holds up the pot.]*

All: Ahhhh. That's beautiful.

Grandmother Spider: With this I will bring back the sun. *[She very slowly walks with the bowl to the tunnel and climbs under.]*

All: Good luck, Grandmother Spider!.

Act 4

[The Sun Guards are out marching around the sun. They are carrying weapons and instruments.]

Narrator: By now the Sun Guards had noticed that someone was trying to steal their sun. These guards were ferocious and ready to fight off anyone or anything. But Grandmother Spider had her size on her side.

Sun Guards: *[Marching around the sun playing their instruments]* Save the sun! Save the sun!!

[Grandmother Spider very slowly climbs out of the tunnel and crawls under the Sun Guards to the sun. She reaches up and takes a piece and then puts it in the pot. She slowly crawls back to the tunnel.]

Narrator: Grandmother Spider went back through the tunnel very slowly. It took a long time for her to crawl back. And all that time the sun was growing in the pot.

Grandmother Spider: *[Crawls out of the tunnel with the sun (a yellow helium balloon) pushing out of the pot.]* I'm back!

All: *[Gathering around her.]* Grandmother Spider, Grandmother Spider!

Grandmother Spider: *[Putting down the pot triumphantly in the middle of the group.]* I have brought you the sun! *[She leans over and releases the balloon into the air. The dark side of the world grows light.]*

Wolf: Thank you, Grandmother Spider! Thank you for bringing us the sun.

Narrator: And from that day on, if you look carefully, you can see the sun in the center of all the webs that Grandmother Spider weaves.

The End

Teacher's Guide

Spreading the Sun

Using the Play

This play could be the centerpiece of a theme about myths or Native Americans. You may also want to consider performing the play as a way to honor Native Americans at Thanksgiving time.

The yellow cardboard sun is a key prop in this play. To make the sun as large as possible, consider constructing it from four large pieces of posterboard that you form into a square, and then cut into the shape of a circle. When you're done with the sun, cut out two pieces as if you're cutting a pie (one for Possum, and one for

Buzzard). Reattach the pieces with Velcro strips so that they can be easily "stolen" during the performance.

Background

Grandmother Spider is known by different names among many Native American tribes. In myths, it is Grandmother Spider who weaves the fabric of the world. It's not surprising that this spider figure is prominent in cultures where the art of weaving is an important and prized skill. In this Cherokee tale, Grandmother Spider invents pottery, and brings the sun to the creatures of the world.

The history of the Cherokee begins years ago near the Great Lakes. After they were defeated by the Iroquois, the Cherokee migrated to the region near the western Carolinas, western Georgia, and eastern Tennessee. Tragically, the Cherokee were forced off of their land as a result of unfair land treaties, and most were relocated to Indian Territory, which is now in Oklahoma. Today there are more than 300,000 Cherokee living in the United States.

Book Links

Your students may enjoy reading more Native American tales and myths.

Dragonfly's Tale by Kristina Rodanas (Clarion Books, 1992)

The First Strawberries: A Cherokee Story by Joseph Bruchac (Dial Books for Young Readers, 1993)

Iktomi and the Berries by Paul Goble (Orchard Books, 1992)

Extending the Play

A Smart Solution

After reading the play, discuss the story with students. Ask: *How did Possum try to steal the sun?* (He tried to hide it in his tail.) *Why didn't that work?* (The sun was so hot it burned his tail.) *How did Buzzard try to steal the sun?* (He tried to hide it in his crown of feathers.) *Why didn't that work?* (The sun was so hot it burned his feathers.) *How did Grandmother Spider try to steal the sun?* (She made a clay pot to hold the sun.) *Why do you think that worked?* (The pot kept the sun from burning her.)

Story Circle

Give students the task of finding another Native American myth to share with the class. (You may wish to recommend some of the titles above, or some of your own favorites.) Then hold a Story Circle in which students retell the tale they liked best to others in the class. By having students retell, instead of reread, the story, you'll be helping them sharpen their summarizing and comprehension skills.

Weaving Wonders

Spiders weave webs. People weave, too. Introduce students to weaving with this simple activity: Cut a number of colored 8 1/2" x 11" pieces of construction paper into 8 1/2" x 1/2" strips. Instruct students to fold another piece of construction paper in half the short way. Students should start at the fold and cut a straight line through the paper, to within about an inch of the border. Students should repeat this to cut six more lines. When you unfold the paper, you will have a basic weaving mat. Have students weave the paper strips over and under the slits in the weaving mat until the paper is filled, then glue the ends of the strips in place. Encourage students to use different colors and experiment with alternating-color patterns.

Making Connections

This play has something in common with "Ossie and the Clever Kinkajou" (p. 148). In both plays, the myths try to explain how some animals acquired physical traits—in this case, the buzzard's bald head and the possum's hairless tail. If you read both plays with your class, see if students can identify the similarities between the two. If you don't read both plays, you still may want to do the animal myth activity on page 156 with this play.

Pecos Bill and Slue-Foot Sue

an American tall tale

adapted by Katherine Noll

Characters

* Narrator #1
* Narrator #2
* Pecos Bill
* Slue-Foot Sue
* Cowboy #1
* Cowboy #2
* Cowboy #3
* Cowgirl #1
* Cowgirl #2

Props

* cowboy hats
* broomstick "horse"
* giant cardboard catfish
* rope

Act 1

Narrator #1: Once upon a time, long ago but not so far away, lived the best cowboy who ever roped a steer. His name was Pecos Bill, and he lived in Texas.

Narrator #2: Pecos Bill was famous in Texas and all of America for his ability to ride and rope. All of the cowboys and cowgirls wanted to be just like him. But Pecos Bill was missing one thing, and that was the perfect horse.

Cowgirl #1: Did you hear the news?

Cowboy #1: What news?

Cowgirl #1: You know those wild horses that roam out on the prairie?

Cowboy #1: Yep, they sure are beautiful. Especially the big white one. He's called Widowmaker. Anyone who's ever tried to ride him has been thrown clear across Texas.

Cowgirl #1: That's what you think. Pecos Bill just went over there. He said he was going to tame Widowmaker and make him his horse.

Cowboy #2: I guess if anyone could tame him it would be Pecos Bill, but I don't know . . .

[Two more cowhands come running in excitedly.]

Cowboy #2: Guess what? Pecos Bill has tamed Widowmaker!

Cowgirl #2: You should have seen it! He spent all day on that horse, and Widowmaker kicked and bucked with all his strength, but Pecos Bill held on. Before the day was over, Widowmaker was as gentle as a kitten.

Cowboy #2: Well, he may have been gentle for Pecos Bill. But I don't think that horse would let anyone else ride him.

[Cowboy #3 enters.]

Cowboy #3: Here comes Pecos Bill riding Widowmaker!

[Pecos Bill enters, riding Widowmaker.]

Pecos Bill: Whoa there! Howdy, everyone!

All cowhands: Howdy, Pecos Bill!

Pecos Bill: I finally found the perfect horse. He's full of spirit and fight. *[Pats Widowmaker.]* Don't worry, old boy, I promise that I'll be the only person to ever ride you.

Narrator #1: From that day on, Pecos Bill and Widowmaker were inseparable. Pecos Bill was more famous than ever now. But he was soon going to meet his match!

Act 2

Pecos Bill and the cowhands are standing by the river.

Cowgirl #2: Bill, is it true you were raised by coyotes?

Pecos Bill: Yep, it sure is true. Till I was ten years old.

Cowboy #2: Is it true you once lassoed a tornado?

Pecos Bill: Yep, that's true, too. I rode that nasty old tornado from one end of Texas to the other.

Cowgirl #2: Wow! Look over there! *[Points offstage.]* Who is that?

Cowboy #3: And what is she doing?

[Slue-Foot Sue enters, "riding" the giant catfish.]

Pecos Bill: Well, I'll be! It's a cowgirl. And she's riding up the river on the back of a giant catfish!

[Sue jumps off the catfish and approaches the cowhands.]

Slue-Foot Sue: Howdy! My name is Slue-Foot Sue.

Pecos Bill: Pleased to meet you. I'm Pecos Bill.

Cowgirl #2: That's some mighty fine riding you were doing.

Cowboy #2: I've never seen anyone ride a catfish before!

Slue-Foot Sue: Aw, that's nothin'! You should see me ride a horse. Let's go rope some cows!

Pecos Bill: Well, all right! Let's go!

[Pecos Bill, Slue-Foot Sue, and the cowhands exit.]

Act 3

Narrator #1: Slue-Foot Sue turned out to be one of the best cowhands in the country. She could ride and rope as well as Bill himself, and every night while Bill and the cowhands sat around the fire, Sue would take out her guitar and play for everyone. Pecos Bill fell in love with Slue-Foot Sue and asked her to marry him. Sue agreed, but only if Bill would let her ride Widowmaker.

Narrator #2: Pecos Bill reluctantly agreed, and after they were married Sue marched right up to that horse and jumped on. Widowmaker was so mad at Pecos Bill for breaking his promise that he kicked and bucked harder than he ever had before. Widowmaker bounced Sue right over the moon! That cured Slue-Foot Sue from ever wanting to ride Bill's horse again. But it turned out to be a good thing that Sue took her trip over the moon, because it helped Sue and Pecos Bill save Texas from a terrible drought.

Pecos Bill: Sue, what are we doing to do? It's so hot that I could fry an egg

on my boots! We need some rain!

Slue-Foot Sue: Well, Bill, I have an idea. Remember when Widowmaker sent me flying over the moon?

Pecos Bill: Sure, how could I forget that?

Slue-Foot Sue: As I was flying over the moon, I noticed that the Big and Little Dippers were filled with water. We have to think of a way to dump that water out all over Texas.

Pecos Bill: Think no more, Sue! Aren't we the best at lassoing in the entire state of Texas?

Slue-Foot Sue: Yep.

Pecos Bill: Well then, let's lasso those dippers! We'll throw our ropes over the handles and pull the dippers till they tip over.

Slue-Foot Sue: Let's do it. We'll have to get up high, though. Let's climb the biggest mountain we can find.

[Bill and Sue look around, then pantomime climbing up a tall mountain. When they reach the top, Bill pulls out a rope.]

Pecos Bill: This ought to do it. Ready, Sue?

Slue-Foot Sue: Ready!

[Pecos Bill swings his rope and throws it up to the sky. Sue grabs the end, and together they start pulling very hard.]

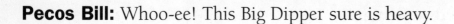

Pecos Bill: Whoo-ee! This Big Dipper sure is heavy.

Slue-Foot Sue: I think it's too heavy. Let's try the Little Dipper.

[Sue swings the rope and throws it up this time. Bill grabs the end, and together they start pulling again.]

Pecos Bill: Just a little more!

Slue-Foot Sue: I think we got it!

[They give one final big tug, and then they drop the rope. Both look up and hold out their hands.]

Slue-Foot Sue: It's raining, Bill! We did it!

Pecos Bill: Yee-ha!

[They dance a little jig. The cowhands come out and start yelling, "Hooray! You did it," etc. They all dance around and celebrate.]

Narrator #1: And that is how Slue-Foot Sue and Pecos Bill ended the drought in Texas. The people of Texas were so grateful they threw a party for Bill and Sue that was said to have lasted for one year. There was plenty of dancing and singing and celebrating!

Narrator #2: In fact, people still remember Pecos Bill and Sue by telling stories of their adventures to this very day. Bill and Sue lived happily ever after, cowhands till the end of their days.

The End

Teacher's Guide

Pecos Bill and Slue-Foot Sue

Using the Play

If staging the play, you may want to set the two narrators off to one side of the stage in chairs. Have the non-performing students sit around them in a circle as though they are listening to storytellers around a campfire, just as cowhands might have done long ago.

Background

As the United States grew and expanded in the 1800s, people began to spin tales of larger-than-life heroes who helped make the country great. Paul Bunyan and John Henry are among the tall tale heroes to emerge during this period. Tall tale heroes always do things in a big way; their achievements, abilities, and even appearances are exaggerated in the tale.

It is commonly believed that Pecos Bill and Slue-Foot Sue were the creation of a writer, Edward O'Reilly, who began chronicling their adventures in 1923 in an attempt to invent the greatest tall tale characters ever. Bill and Sue also have their roots in Texas and cowboy culture. The cattle industry developed in the 1860s in Texas, when cowhands would lead cattle on long drives to rail lines in Kansas, Nebraska, and Wyoming.

Book Links

American Tall Tales by Mary Pope Osborne (Knopf, 1991)

Cowboy by David H. Murdoch (Dorling Kindersley, 1992)

Outrageous, Bodacious Boliver Boggs by Jo Harper (Simon & Schuster, 1996)

Extending the Play

Word Watch

Students may benefit from a vocabulary review before reading this play.

cowhand: a worker who kept watch over the cattle on long cattle drives

drought: a long period of time where there is no rain

inseparable: when two people or things are always together

lasso: a rope with a loop at one end that tightens when the rope is pulled

steer: a young male member of the cattle family

What Makes a Tale Tall?

Before reading the play, ask students if they know what a tall tale is. Can they guess from the name what kind of tale it may be? Explain that exaggeration is used to tell a story. An exaggerated story is based on truth, but it enlarges some of the details to make the story more incredible.

After reading the play, ask students to point out the exaggerated details. (Slue-Foot Sue was such a good rider she could ride a catfish; Pecos Bill was such a good cowhand he could lasso the stars; the Big Dipper and the Little Dipper are full of water.)

Ask students to use what they know about exaggeration to invent their own tall tale characters. Students should decide what special things their character can do, and then give some exaggerated examples of

their characters' abilities. For example, they may invent a runner who can run so fast, she can circle the world in a day. Brainstorm some characters and abilities with students before they work on their assignments.

More to the Story

This play only tells about some of the adventures of Pecos Bill and Slue-Foot Sue. Challenge students to find another tale about either of these cowhands. As a class, adapt the tale into another act in the play and add it to your next performance or reading.

The Big and Little Dippers

In the tall tale, the Big Dipper and the Little Dipper are described as being filled with water! These two star groupings are among the easiest to spot in the night sky. Almost everyone has seen the Big Dipper; the Little Dipper is easy to spot if you know this trick: Find the two stars on the right side of the dipper's bowl. Follow an imaginary straight line extending up from these two stars. They point to the North Star, which is the first star on the Little Dipper's handle.

You may wish to instruct students to try to spot these constellations at night, with a parent's help. The best spots for viewing the stars are away from tall buildings and bright lights.

How the Rainbow Was Born

a Zapotec myth

adapted by Carol Pugliano-Martin

Characters

* Narrator #1
* Narrator #2
* Lightning
* Cloud Keeper
* Rain Keeper

* Hail Keeper
* Wind Keeper
* People (one or more as needed)
* Animals (one or more as needed)
* Sun

Act 1

Narrator #1: Long ago, there was no light. The people and the animals lived in the dark.

Narrator #2: Sun and his younger cousin, Lightning, lived in the sky. Sun ruled over the Cloud Keeper, the Rain Keeper, the Hail Keeper, and the Wind Keeper.

Narrator #1: Each Keeper had a big clay pot. Sun had ordered the Keepers to keep their pots closed. The Keepers obeyed Sun. The pots had never been opened.

Narrator #2: One day, while Sun was away, Lightning decided to be in charge. Lightning surprised everyone with a command.

Lightning: Cloud Keeper! Open your pot! Let out the clouds!

Cloud Keeper: Really? Are you sure?

Lightning: Yes, I am sure.

Cloud Keeper: Well, OK. Here they come!

Narrator #1: Cloud Keeper opened the lid of the pot. Giant gray clouds came tumbling out of the pot. They filled the sky.

Narrator #2: Lightning and Cloud Keeper were very excited by what they

saw. They began to dance in the sky. Bolts of lightning came from Lightning's fingertips as he danced around.

[Lightning and Cloud Keeper dance around happily. Lightning pantomimes lightning coming out of his fingers. They both make stormlike sounds.]

People: *[Looking up.]* Wow! Look at that! The clouds and lightning are so beautiful!

Animals: But we are so thirsty. It would be nice if we could have some rain.

Narrator #1: Lightning heard this.

Narrator #2: He turned to the Rain Keeper and spoke.

Lightning: Rain Keeper! Open your pot! Let out the rain!

Rain Keeper: Really? Are you sure?

Lightning: Yes. I am sure.

Rain Keeper: Well, OK. Here it comes!

Narrator #1: Rain Keeper opened the lid of the pot. Cool, wet rain fell on the earth.

Narrator #2: Lightning, Cloud Keeper, and Rain Keeper were very excited by what they saw. They began to dance. More clouds, more lightning, and

lots of rain filled the sky.

[Lightning, Cloud Keeper, and Rain Keeper dance around happily, making appropriate storm sounds.]

People: The rain helped us to not be thirsty anymore. But now it is getting scary down here.

Animals: Let's go up there and ask them if they will stop all this.

Act 2

[Some people and animals walk up to the sky.]

People: Oh, Great Sun . . . *[Looking around for Sun.]* Hey, where is Sun?

Lightning: He's away. I'm in charge for today.

People: Oh, OK. Lightning, we are here to ask you . . .

Narrator #1: Suddenly the people and the animals noticed the two pots that hadn't been opened.

Animals: Hey, what's in these two pots? Will you open them?

Lightning: Well . . . I don't know. I've already done more than I should have today.

People and Animals: Oh, pleeeeaaassse!

Lightning: Well, OK. After all, I am the boss today. Hail Keeper! Open your pot! Let out the hail!

Hail Keeper: Really? Are you sure?

Lightning: Yes. I am sure.

Hail Keeper: Well, OK. Here it comes!

Narrator #2: Hail Keeper opened the lid of the pot. Giant hailstones fell from the sky. Lightning, Cloud Keeper, Rain Keeper, and Hail Keeper were very excited by what they saw. They all began to dance.

[Lightning, Cloud Keeper, Rain Keeper, and Hail Keeper dance around happily, making appropriate storm sounds.]

Narrator #1: The storm got stronger and stronger. It scared the people and the animals. They ran back to the earth.

People: This is terrible! It feels like it is the end of the world! What can we do?

Narrator #2: At that moment, Sun returned. He heard the cries of the people and the animals.

Sun: I will help you, my friends. *(To Lightning.)* Lightning, what have you been doing while I was away? Now I know what can happen when you are

left alone!

Lightning: *[Quietly.]* Uh-oh.

[The Sun, acting big and strong, approaches the others. They move closer to each other and stop dancing around.]

Sun: You! Wind Keeper! Open your pot! Let out the wind!

Narrator #1: Wind Keeper did not ask if Sun was sure. He knew he was.

[Wind Keeper opens his pot and makes wind noises and motions, driving all of the others away.]

Narrator #2: The other Keepers returned to their places beside their pots.

Lightning: Sun, I am sorry for the trouble I have caused. You are the real leader of the sky. I would like to give you a gift as an apology.

[Lightning closes his eyes and moves his arms around.]

Narrator #1: Suddenly, a beautiful band of colors filled the sky. There was red, the color of ripe apples. There was orange, the color of carrots.

Narrator #2: There was yellow, the color of sunflowers. There was green, the color of grass.

Narrator #1: There was blue, the color of the sky. There was indigo, the

color of a ripe blueberry.

Narrator #2: And there was violet, the color of juicy grapes.

People and Animals: *[Pointing up at the sky.]* Ooooooohhhhhh!

Lightning: Sun, here is a bridge from the sky to the earth. You can climb over the bridge to share your light with the people and animals. They will no longer have to live in darkness.

All: And this is how the rainbow was born.

The End

Teacher's Guide

How the Rainbow Was Born

Using the Play

If you choose to perform the play, it's possible that all of your students can take on acting roles. After assigning the major roles, divide the rest of the class into "people" and "animals."

This play also provides many opportunities for creative costuming. Ask students to imagine what a Cloud Keeper wears (a cape made of cotton balls?); what Lightning wears (a shirt with paper lightning rods pinned to it?), etc. Students playing people could research the types of clothing that the Zapotec people wore, and students playing animals could find out what kinds of animals live in Mexico and create appropriate animal masks.

Background

This play fits nicely into a number of themes: a science theme about rainbows, a folk tale theme, or a theme about Mexico. Here are some basic facts to help you with these options:

Rainbows

Even though the story of how the rainbow was born is a myth, this play contains one factual element, the seven colors of the rainbow: red, orange, yellow, green, blue, indigo, and violet.

In nature, a rainbow occurs when the sun shines on falling rain. The raindrops act like a prism and break up the light into seven bands of color. These bands of color form a complete circle, but we can't see the other half below the horizon.

The Zapotec people

This play is adapted from a myth of the ancient Zapotec people of Mexico, who created an advanced civilization in what is today Oaxaca City. At its peak, the Zapotec city of Monte Albán had a population of 66,000, a system of hieroglyphics, and numerous temples and tombs. The civilization was eventually absorbed by the Aztec empire. Today, the Zapotec people still live in Oaxaca.

Book Links

From rainbows to Zapotec myths and facts.

Beneath the Stone: A Mexican Zapotec Tale by Bernard Wolf (Orchard Books, 1994)

Sparky's Rainbow Repair by Max Haynes (Lothrop, Lee and Shephard, 1992)

The Tale of Rabbit and Coyote by Tony Johnston and Tomie dePaola (Paper Star, 1998)

The Woman Who Outshone the Sun: The Legend of Lucia Zenteno/La Mujer Que Brillaba Más Que El Sol: La Leyenda de Lucia Zenteno by Alejandro Cruz Martinez (Children's Book Press, 1998)

Extending the Play

Color Fun

Before reading this play, you may wish to introduce students to the mnemonic device ROY G BIV to help students remember the seven colors of the rainbow: red, orange, yellow, green, blue, indigo, and violet. Explain that indigo is a deep, rich shade of blue. Younger students could go on a color hunt in the classroom and identify items that match these seven colors.

During the color hunt, children will notice many varieties of these color shades. Explain that colors can be mixed together to form new colors. This can be demonstrated with finger paints in three colors: red, yellow, and blue. Challenge students to mix the colors together, a little at a time, to create new colors. They should keep a record of the colors they make on a separate sheet of paper. What colors have they created? What names would they give their colors? Can they use the paints to make all of the colors in the rainbow? Introduce black and white paint so that students can make their colors darker or lighter.

Somewhere Over the Rainbow

What's at the end of the rainbow? A pot of gold? A strange new land? This question has captivated the minds of people since the first rainbow was sighted. Have children imagine what may be at the end of a rainbow, draw a picture of it, and write about it.

Where in the World?

Inform students that this tale originated in what is today Oaxaca City, Mexico. Challenge students to use a map of North America to answer the following questions:

Which U.S. states border Mexico?

Which bodies of water border Mexico?

In what direction would you travel to go from our city to Oaxaca City?

How many states would you travel through on your trip?

How many miles would you travel?

How many bodies of water would you cross?

What do you think the weather may be like in Oaxaca City?

Ossie and the Clever Kinkajou

adapted by Robin Bernard

Characters

* Narrator
* Ossie the yellow cat
* Horace & Harry, howler monkeys
* Sophie Sloth
* Arnie Armadillo
* Caleb Crocodile
* Boris Bush Pig
* Tessa Tapir
* The Clever Kinkajou

Props

* paper leaves and vines
* green/brown paper river
* paper-bag animal masks
* stick-on "spots"
* pin-on tail for Ossie
* wooden bowl with "food"

Act 1

A clearing in the rain forest near the river. A crocodile is sunning himself on the bank. Two howler monkeys, Horace and Harry, are at the edge of the water, drinking along with the other animals.

Narrator: In the rain forest many years ago, there lived a yellow cat. He was long, and he was tall, but he was very, very thin . . .

[Ossie enters. His head is down, and he looks tired and sad .]

Horace: *[To Harry.]* Would you look at Ossie! Every time I see him he looks skinnier!

Harry: *[To Horace.]* Maybe he's on a diet.

Horace: *[In a stage whisper.]* Arnie Armadillo told me that for a cat, he's a terrible hunter! He hardly catches a thing!

Caleb: Hi, Ossie! How are you today?

Ossie: Not too good, Caleb Crocodile. The only thing I caught all morning was a beetle! Everything else saw me coming and ran away.

Caleb: Oh my, oh my, oh my, that's not good. But, Ossie, have you thought of telling your problems to the clever kinkajou? Perhaps *he* could help you.

Ossie: Do you really think so? I've tried everything else and I'm still the worst hunting cat in the rain forest—and the hungriest!

[Enter Arnie Armadillo.]

Arnie: Hi, Ossie. I overheard what you said, and I can tell you that the kinkajou helped me a whole lot. He showed me how to roll into a ball to protect myself.

[Enter Sophie Sloth.]

Sophie: He helped me, too, Ossie. He told me to stop cleaning my fur and let the algae grow in it. Now nobody can spot me hanging from a branch!

Ossie: I don't think *anybody* can help me, Sophie, but I'll go talk with the kinkajou anyway.

[Ossie starts walking away from the river into the forest.]

Horace & Harry: Good luck, Ossie!

Caleb & Sophie: Good luck, Ossie!

Arnie: Good luck, Ossie!

Act 2

Another part of the forest.

Tessa: Greetings, Ossie. Where are you going?

Ossie: Hi, Tessa Tapir. I'm off to find the clever kinkajou. Have you seen him?

Tessa: I sure have, Ossie. He just helped me solve a big problem. You know how often I'd bite my nose by mistake whenever I ate? Well, the kinkajou just showed me how to get it out of the way! He's right over there, resting under the mango tree.

[Tessa exits, and Ossie walks up to the kinkajou.]

Ossie: Er . . . excuse me, clever kinkajou, but I need your help. You see, I have a strange problem, for a cat . . . .

Kinkajou: Come, sit down and rest, Ossie. And have something to eat. *[The kinkajou sets down a bowl of food which Ossie eats hungrily.]* I'm glad you've come to see me because I know about your problem.

Ossie: You do?

Kinkajou: Of course! You are a very skinny cat. I can see that you are having a hard time catching anything to eat.

Ossie: That's right!

Kinkajou: I can tell just by looking at you what the problem is. And I know how to solve it.

Ossie: Oh, kinkajou, *please* tell me!

Kinkajou: I will, Ossie, but first promise me that you'll do exactly what I say, even if it sounds strange.

Ossie: Oh, I will kinkajou, I promise!

Kinkajou: Then listen closely to what I'm going to tell you, Ossie . . .

[Ossie and the kinkajou have their backs to the audience. Ossie moves closer and the kinkajou whispers in his ear.]

#

* Scene 1 *

Ossie is back at the river. Boris, a huge bush pig, is drinking at the river's edge. He does not see Ossie. Ossie takes a few nervous steps toward Boris, then backs away. He tries again, but backs away again. The third time, he sneaks up right behind Boris.

Ossie: *[Loudly and bravely.]* Ugh! What an ugly beast you are! You must be

the ugliest animal in the rain forest!

Boris: How dare you, you scrawny cat! I'll teach you some manners.

Narrator: Boris charged Ossie and tossed him into the muddy river.

[Boris stomps away. Ossie crawls out of the river.]

Ossie: Whew! That was scary! And I have mud spots all over me. *[Yawning]* But I'm too tired to wash myself now. Maybe later . . . *[He falls asleep.]*

* Scene 2 *

*Ossie wakes up and stretches. He shakes himself several times to loosen the mud spots, but they don't come off. He tries to lick himself clean, but the spots won't come off. **He is now a spotted cat.***

Ossie: What is this? I wash and I wash and these spots won't come off! You know, they don't look so bad.

[All of the animals enter.]

Horace: Oh, look at you, Ossie! Your new coat is beautiful!

Sophie: I love your spots, Ossie!

Arnie: Wow! Even your tail looks great!

Harry: Try hunting *now*, Ossie. Your new spots look just like rain forest shadows. You'll blend right in, and nobody will see you coming!

Caleb: Cool, Ossie! You'll be a great hunter!

Ossie: You're right! I bet these spots will work! This is probably just what the kinkajou planned.

Narrator: And that's how Ossie became the spotted hunting cat we call an ocelot, and he never went hungry again.

The End

Teacher's Guide

Ossie and the Clever Kinkajou

Using the Play

If you choose to stage this play, creating some kind of paper "river" for your set will really help to organize the actors on stage. In Acts 1 and 3, the actors can easily gather by the river, and it will also help to divide the stage so that the "other part of the forest" is clear in Act 2.

Even if your students read the play, you may still wish to have students make paper animal masks to represent their characters and other rain forest animals. Students can also research rain forest plants, make them using colorful paper, and decorate the classroom with them.

Background

The animals in this play can all be found in a tropical rain forest.

* **Ocelot:** This member of the feline family is deep yellow and has black spots. It feeds on small mammals, snakes, and birds.

* **Howler monkey:** This reddish brown monkey lives in the tree branches, or canopy, of the rain forest. It gets its name from the loud noise it makes to protect its territory.

* **Sloth:** This canopy dweller clings to tree branches with its long claws. The green algae in its fur helps it to hide from predators while it eats leaves and flowers in the trees.

* **Armadillo:** This animal was named "small armored one" because it is covered with bony plates over much of its body. It mostly feeds on small animals such as frogs, snakes, and insects.

* **Crocodile:** These reptiles spend most of their lives in water. Broad-snouted crocodiles, such as you might find in a tropical rain forest, chiefly eat frogs, birds, and small mammals.

* **Tapir:** (pronounced TAY-puhr): This mammal has hooves and a snout, making it look like a pig. However, its closest cousins are the rhinoceros and the horse.

* **Bush pig:** The shy bush pig is not often seen by humans in the wild, and prefers to come out at night.

* **Kinkajou:** It's sometimes called a honey bear because it loves to eat honey, but the kinkajou is a member of the raccoon family.

Book Links

Bitter Bananas by Isaac Olaleye (Boyds Mills Press, 1994)

The Great Kapok Tree, a Tale of the Amazon Rain Forest by Lynne Cherry (Harcourt Brace, 1990)

One Day in a Tropical Rain Forest by Jean Craighead George (HarperCollins, 1995)

Extending the Play

On the Hunt

After reading the play, discuss the story with students. Ask: *Why was Ossie hungry in the beginning of the play?* (He couldn't hunt animals with his bright yellow coat; they could see him coming.) *What did the Clever Kinkajou tell Ossie to do?* (Go to the river and make Boris angry.) *What happened after Boris pushed Ossie into the river?* (Ossie's yellow coat became spotted with mud.) *Why do you think it would be easier to hunt for animals with a spotted coat?* (The spotted coat will help

Ossie blend into the forest.)

Point out that an ocelot is an animal that hunts for its food. These hunting animals are called predators. Can students name other animal predators?

Animal Tales

In this play, we find out how the ocelot got his spots. This type of myth is common to many cultures. Your students can create their own myths using this format: How the _____ Got Its _____.

Have students choose a rain forest animal, pick a distinguishing feature of the animal, and then imagine how the animal may have gotten that feature in writing or through pictures. You may wish to use some of these ideas:

How the Armadillo Got Its Armor

How the Peccary Got Its Collar

How the Kinkajou Got Its Tail

How the Howler Monkey Got Its Howl

Rain Forest Riddle Book

Challenge students with this riddle:

Green algae grows in my fur coat. It helps me hide from predators in the tree branches. I am the _____ .

Can students guess the answer? (the sloth) Challenge students to make their own riddles. Ask them to write their riddles on the front of a piece of paper and then draw the animal and write its name on the back of the paper. Collect all the riddles and use a three-hole punch to turn them into a "Rain Forest Riddle Book."

Getting to Know You

by Tracey West

Welcome Back to School

Characters

* Teacher
* Students

Setting

* Your classroom

The teacher sits at the front of the class and addresses her students, who are seated.

Teacher: Welcome, students.
The year is new.
Now I'd like
to get to know you.

Students: Get to know us
name by name.
Sometimes we're different.
Sometimes we're the same.

Teacher: Hmm. Let's see. Let's talk about our families.
If you have a brother, put your hand in the air.
If you don't have a brother, leave your hand right there.

[Students respond to the rhyme.]

Teacher: Let's try another.
If you have a sister, put your hand in the air.
If you don't have a sister, leave your hand right there.

[Students respond to the rhyme.]

Teacher: That was great! But I'd like to know more.
Welcome, students.
The year is new.
Now I'd like
to get to know you.

Students: Get to know us
name by name.
Sometimes we're different.
Sometimes we're the same.

Teacher: If you have a pet, put your hand in the air.
If you don't have a pet, leave your hand right there.

[Students respond to the rhyme.]

Teacher: Now I think I'd like to know what you like to do.
If you like to watch TV, put your hand in the air.
If you don't like TV, leave your hand right there.

[Students respond to the rhyme.]

Teacher: Let's try another one.
If you like to play sports, put your hand in the air.
If you don't like sports, leave your hand right there.

[Students respond to the rhyme.]

Teacher: How about one more?
If you like to draw pictures, put your hand in the air.
If you don't like draw, leave your hand right there.

Teacher: That was great! But I'd still like to know more.
Welcome, students.
The year is new.

Now I'd like
to get to know you.

Students: Get to know us
name by name.
Sometimes we're different.
Sometimes we're the same.

Teacher: Now I think I'd like to know what your favorite colors are.
Listen carefully:
If your favorite color is blue, stand up.
If your favorite color is red, sit down.
If your favorite color is yellow, give me a smile.
If your favorite color is green, give me a frown.
If your favorite color is black, raise one hand.
If your favorite color is pink, raise two.
If I didn't say your favorite color,
Then tell me when I call on you.

[Students respond to the rhyme. The teacher looks for those who haven't responded and asks them to tell what their favorite colors are.]

Teacher: That was fun! I have one more rhyme before we're done:
Welcome, students.
I want to thank you
for helping me
to get to know you!

The End

Teacher's Guide

Getting to Know You

Using the Play

This interactive play was designed to be simple enough to perform during the hectic first days of school, and it can be performed by all students, no matter what their reading abilities.

Before starting the play, write the students' rhyme on the board. Say the rhyme with students. Let students know that you'll be performing a play together. When you point to the board, students should repeat the rhyme. Students should also listen carefully, because you'll be asking them to respond to you during the play.

Background

It's hard to match the jitters and excitement that students—and teachers—experience on the first day of school. For many students, all of the new people they meet are a big part of that excitement. It's also a big part of their nervousness, too. New people can be a little scary until we get to know them.

By performing this play, you and your students will get to know one another a little better. Students will also gain practice in movement and following directions.

Don't let the written script limit your experience with the play. If there are other things you'd like to find out about your students, ask the question and use the basic hand-raising rhyme. (If you like _____, raise your hand in the air, if you don't like _____ leave your hand right there.)

Book Links

Amanda Pig, Schoolgirl by Jean van Leeuwen (Dial Books for Young Readers, 1997)

Amber Brown Goes Fourth by Paula Danziger (Putnam, 1995)

Hello, First Grade by Joanne Ryder (Troll, 1993)

How to Survive First Grade by Laurie Lawler (Albert Whitman & Co., 1998)

Extending the Play

Flip-Up Fun

It's easy to make a flip-up bulletin board with a "Getting to Know You" theme. To start, cut out letters and attach the words *Get to Know Us* across the top of the board. In the center of the board, write out the students' rhyme from the play.

For each student, fold a piece of plain paper in half (11" x 17" paper works best). Trace a circle on the paper, making sure one edge of the circle falls on the fold. Have students cut out the circles.

Each student should draw a picture of his or her face on the top circle. Then instruct students to lift up the flap and write their names and some things about them on the inside of the flap. Attach the circles to the bulletin board so that visitors can lift up the flaps and learn more about the students in your class.

Personal Interviews

Divide the class into pairs. Ask students to take turns interviewing one another. Students should be encouraged to ask questions such as:

How many people are in your family?

What is your favorite subject in school?

What is your favorite hobby?

Do you have any pets?

What is your favorite food?

Have you always lived in this town?

Suggest that students take notes during the interview so that they don't forget anything. When the interviews are finished, have students write up their information on a page titled "All About _____ ." Older students can be encouraged to turn their information into a personality profile, such as they may read in a magazine.

Getting-to-Know-You Graphs

The questions in the play make a great springboard to math activities. When the play is over, repeat the questions again. This time, tally students' responses with the aid of student helpers. Write the results on the chalkboard.

You can use these results to create simple graphs. For example, take the question about who has a brother. Divide a large piece of paper in half. Across the top of one side, write "Students who have a brother." Across the other side, write "Students who don't have a brother." Have students write their names on small stick-on notes and then stick the note to the appropriate side. Which side has more notes? You should be able to tell just by looking at the graph.

Make Up Your Mind, Marvin

by Tracey West

Marvin walks into Sally Century's "100 Flavors" Ice Cream Shop. Sally and her helpers are there.

Sally: *[To helpers.]* Oh, no! Here comes Marvin. He can never make up his mind.

Marvin: Hi, Sally.

Sally: Hi, Marvin.

Marvin: I'm in the mood for some ice cream today, but I don't know what flavor I want.

Sally: How about vanilla, Marvin? That's what you always get.

Marvin: Maybe, but I think today I'd like to try something new. Why don't you remind me what your one hundred flavors are?

Sally: *[Sighs.]* Not again. Okay, Marvin. *[In a singsong voice.]* Presenting Sally Century's one hundred flavors! We've got vanilla, chocolate, strawberry, banana, peanut butter, chocolate chip, mint chocolate chip, butterscotch, cookie dough, and rocky road.

Marvin: Hmm. That's only ten flavors. Don't you have any more?

Helper #1: We've got raspberry, blueberry, blackberry, elderberry, gooseberry, cranberry, berry swirl, very berry, double berry, and cherry berry.

Marvin: Nope. None of those sound quite right. Besides, that's only twenty flavors.

Helper #2: How about peach, mango, guava, papaya, pineapple, kiwi, lemon, lime, coconut, or tutti-frutti?

Marvin: That sounds *too* fruity for me! Anyway, that's only thirty.

Helper #3: How about praline, almond, pistachio, walnut, banana nut, macadamia nut, crunchy nut, caramel nut, chunky nut, or butter pecan?

Marvin: Those flavors are too nutty for me! That's only forty flavors, you know.

Helper #4: How about chocolate fudge, vanilla fudge, pumpkin fudge, fudge swirl, fudge ripple, nutty fudge, brownie fudge, marshmallow fudge, mocha fudge, or fudge surprise?

Marvin: They all sound so good! And that's only fifty so far.

Sally: [*To helpers.*] At least we're halfway through!

Helper #1: You'll love our international flavors, Marvin. There's French vanilla, English toffee, Dutch chocolate, German chocolate, Swiss chocolate, Italian ice, Mexican marshmallow, Russian raisin, Turkish Taffy, and Swedish strawberry.

Marvin: Hmm. I just don't know. All sixty flavors sound good.

Helper #2: You can't go wrong with our crunchy flavors. There's vanilla crunch, chocolate crunch, caramel crunch, peanut crunch, candy crunch, cookie crunch, graham cracker crunch, coconut crunch, and crunchy crunch.

Marvin: I don't know. I just went to the dentist. Besides, that's only seventy.

Helper #3: Everyone loves our candy flavors. There's bubble gum, licorice, lollipop, gummy bear, peppermint stick, jelly bean, sugarplum, chocolate truffle, candy bar, and candy supreme.

Marvin: They sound sweet. But I still can't make up my mind! And you've only told me about eighty flavors.

Helper #4: Our double flavors are twice as nice! How about double chocolate, double fudge, double nut, double bubble gum, double delight, double berry, double brownie, double fruity, double marshmallow, or our most dangerous flavor, double trouble?

Marvin: Now I'm twice as confused as before! Besides, that's only ninety. Don't you have ten more flavors?

Sally: [Sighs.] This is it, Marvin. Our last ten flavors are our freaky flavors. There's avocado, rhubarb, violet, prickly pear, pawpaw, pineapple pesto, seaweed, anchovy, garlic, and broccoli. That's one hundred flavors.

Marvin: Oh, my. I just can't seem to make up my mind.

Sally: Please, Marvin. We've told you all one hundred flavors. What kind of ice cream do you want?

Marvin: *[Hesitating.]* Well, I think . . .

Helpers: Yes?

Marvin: I think I'll have . . .

Helpers: Make up your mind, Marvin!

Marvin: OK, I know what I'll have.

Sally: What?

Marvin: I'll have vanilla, please!

Sally and Helpers: Oh, Marvin!

The End

Teacher's Guide

Make Up Your Mind, Marvin

Using the Play

If you choose to perform the play, Sally and her helpers may have a hard time memorizing their lines. A fun solution is to have your prop crew make up signs for each group of ten flavors (Classic Flavors, Nutty Flavors, etc.) and post them on the wall of Sally Century's 100 Flavors. That way, the actors can read off the ice cream flavors from the signs.

Background

Each year, teachers all over the country celebrate the 100th day of school. The purpose of the celebration is twofold: to give students a sense of pride and accomplishment in their achievements so far, and to explore the number 100.

This play can be the focus of your class's "100 Days" celebration, and also act as a springboard for activities that can be performed on the day as well.

Book Links

The 100th Day of School by Angela Shelf Medearis (Cartwheel Books, 1996)

One Hundred Hungry Ants by Eleanor Pinczes (Houghton Mifflin, 1993)

One Hundred Is a Family by Pam Munoz Ryan (Hyperion, 1994)

To School and Beyond! by Judy Katschke (Disney Press, 1998)

Extending the Play

100 Flavors

In the play, Sally Century and her helpers read off the names of the 100 flavors in groups of 10. During a reading of the play, stop after each group and ask: How many flavors are left?

Write each flavor on an index card to create multipurpose manipulatives. Keep the flavor cards at a learning center. Also create activity cards for children to choose and then use with the flavor cards. Some sample activities could include:

Sort the cards in alphabetical order.

Put the cards in groups of 5. Then count by 5s. How many cards are there?

Put the cards in groups of 10. Then count by 10s. How many cards are there?

Put the cards in groups of 20. How many groups are there?

Put the cards in groups of 25. How many groups are there?

Sort the cards into two piles. In one pile, put flavors you would like to try. In another pile, put flavors you would not like to try. Count each pile by ones. Use the numbers to make an equation that equals 100.

Brainstorming Fun

Divide the class into two groups. Ask one group to imagine that Sally Century has opened up a zoo called "Sally Century's 100 Animals." Ask another group to imagine that Sally has opened up a travel agency called "Sally Century's 100 Places to Visit." Challenge the groups to brainstorm and make a list of 100 animals/places. Encourage students to turn to books in the classroom to help with their research. When the two lists are finished, you can turn the animals and places into manipulatives and use them at a learning center as well.

Celebrate 100 Days

If you don't currently celebrate the 100th day of school, why not start? If you have Internet access, do a subject search under "100 Days of School" to find lots of great ideas from teachers around the country.

Here are some simple things you can do to make your celebration special:

* To build excitement, begin a countdown on the first day of school, counting back from 100.

* Asks students to bring in 100 objects from home, such as paper clips, pennies, pieces of breakfast cereal, mini-marshmallows, etc. (Or divide the class into groups of 5 and ask each student to bring in 20, etc.) Use the objects at math stations where students can practice counting to 100 in a variety of ways.

* Challenge children to find 100 mathematical ways to express 100.

* Have a party featuring 100 of each kind of refreshment: 100 cupcakes, 100 miniature candy bars, 100 carrot sticks, etc.

* Have children keep track of books they read during the year, in school and at home. As a class, brainstorm a list of 100 books you have read. Follow this with a read-aloud book about the number 100 or the 100th day of school.

For more ideas, you may wish to check out *The Celebrate 100 Kit* (Scholastic, 1998), which contains *The 100th Day of School* by Angela Shelf Medearis and *The Celebrate 100 Activity Book* by Mary Spann, along with stickers, a poster, and a cassette tape.

The Riddle Bee

by Jennifer Johnson

Can you guess the answer?

Characters

* Miss Ward (teacher)
* Jeremy
* Selena
* Jackie
* Megan
* Kyle
* Manolo
* other students

Props

* desks or chairs for students
* guinea pigs (small stuffed animals) in cage

Act 1

A classroom. Kids are seated; the teacher is at the front of the class.

Miss Ward: Hi, everyone. Welcome to your last day of school. I know all of you are feeling very sad about a whole summer away from school, right?

[Laughs and groans from students.]

Miss Ward: We've got a lot of things going on today. Later on, of course, there's our party with Ms. Leslie's class.

[Cheers from students.]

Miss Ward: But right now, we've got something to take care of. Can anyone guess what I'm talking about?

Jeremy: You're going to tell us our grades?

Miss Ward: Good guess, Jeremy, but I won't hand out report cards until the end of the day.

Selena: I know! The guinea pigs. We have to decide who's taking Tony and Mugwump.

Miss Ward: Exactly! . . . sort of. Actually, I've already decided that Manolo can take home Tony. He's done the very best job of taking care of the guinea pigs this year.

Manolo: Thanks, Miss Ward.

Miss Ward: But Mugwump still needs a home.

[Students shout things like "Me!" and "I'll take her!"]

Miss Ward: Settle down, guys. *No one's* taking Mugwump without a permission slip. Come on up if you've got one.

[Jeremy, Selena, Jackie, and Kyle turn in slips.]

Miss Ward: Hmm . . . four permission slips and one guinea pig. We need to decide who gets Mugwump. Here's how we're going to do it. You know how sometimes we have a spelling bee? Today, we're going to have a riddle bee! The one who answers the most riddles wins.

Act 2

Jeremy, Selena, Jackie, and Kyle are standing up, lined up against a wall. Others are still sitting in their seats. Teacher is standing at the front of the class.

Miss Ward: Okay, guys, are you ready to begin?

Riddle-bee kids: *[All together, loudly.]* Ready!

Miss Ward: We'll do it like a spelling bee. As long as you get the right answer, you're in. But as soon you give a wrong answer . . . you're outta

here—until we narrow it down to two players. Okay, Jeremy, this one's for you. What did the moose call his girlfriend?

Jeremy: The moose? Let's see. *[Chuckles.]* I guess he called her "deer."

Miss Ward: Excellent! *[Clapping and cheering from students.]* Jackie, you're next. What kind of jewelry does a rabbit wear?

Jackie: That's easy. Fourteen *carrot* gold, of course.

Miss Ward: Good answer, Jackie. Selena, here's a tough one. Where are the Great Plains located?

Selena: That's not so tough. The *great planes* are located in the big airports!

Miss Ward: You passed with flying colors! Okay, Kyle, what makes the Tower of Pisa lean?

Kyle: *[Confused.]* What makes pizza lean? Umm . . . too much pepperoni on one side?

[Snickering from students.]

Miss Ward: Sorry, Kyle. That was a good try, though.

[Kyle walks to his seat with his head down, sad.]

Miss Ward: Jeremy, back to you. What makes the Tower of Pisa *lean?*

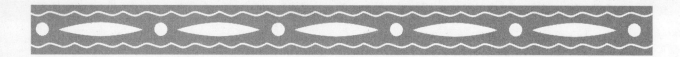

Jeremy: I know. It never eats.

Miss Ward: You've got that straight! Jackie, what has keys that have no locks?

Jackie: Keys . . . keys. I know. A piano!

Miss Ward: Jackie, I think you've got the *answer* key! Speaking of keys, Selena, how do you unlock a cemetery gate?

Selena: [Stumped.] Hmm . . .. I don't know. . . . a *scary* key?

Miss Ward: Sorry, Selena. I'm afraid you just locked yourself out!

[Selena stomps to her seat, annoyed.]

Miss Ward: Jeremy? Do you know what unlocks a cemetery gate?

Jeremy: *[Grinning.]* A skeleton key, of course!

Miss Ward: Guess you really *boned up* on your riddles, Jeremy! *[Clapping from students.]* Okay, Jackie, what kind of food do you eat in the desert?

Jackie: *[Grinning.] Sand*wiches, naturally.

Miss Ward: You must be eating brain food! Jeremy, what kind of paper grows on trees?

Jackie: [*Looking nervous.*] Hmm . . . . Let's see. . . [*Slowly, frowning.*] Paper? On trees? . . . Oh, wow. Ummm. . . *green* paper?

Miss Ward: Sorry, Jeremy. But you're not out yet. First, Jackie has to answer the riddle correctly. Jackie?

Jackie: [*With a big smile.*] *Loose-leaf* paper grows on trees.

Miss Ward: Kids, we've got a winner! Jackie, you can claim your prize after the party.

[*Class applauds Jackie.*]

Manolo: I'll be right there, Miss Ward. I want to make sure all of Mugwump's things are packed for Jackie.

Act 3

Class troops back into classroom, following the party. Manolo is already in the classroom, by the guinea pig cage.

Selena: Hey, Manolo, where were you? You missed the party.

Manolo: I just couldn't leave Tony and Mugwump. They were playing together and having a good time. I think Tony's going to miss Mugwump.

Miss Ward: Speaking of Mugwump, I think it's time for Jackie to come on up to the front of the class and claim her summer prize.

Jackie: Thanks, Miss Ward. But the thing is, I'm not going to take Mugwump after all. If you don't mind, there's someone else I'd like to give her to.

Miss Ward: Well, all right, Jackie, but what's up? You won Mugwump fair and square.

Jackie: Yeah, I know. *[Smiles.]* I was really *good* in that riddle bee! But I'm thinking it's not right to split up Tony and Mugwump. They might be really sad if we do that. And Manolo really knows how to take care of those guinea pigs. I want him to have them both.

[Sounds of approval from students.]

Miss Ward: Manolo? How's that sound to you?

Manolo: Sounds totally cool, Miss Ward. I've been worrying about them getting lonely.

Miss Ward: All right, then. Manolo will take Tony *and* Mugwump. I'll bet they will be happier together. And Jackie, I must say, I'm really impressed by your decision.

Selena: Way to go, Jackie.

Jeremy: Yeah, that was really cool.

Miss Ward: That reminds me of another riddle. What's cool and hot at the same time?

All kids: Summertime!

Miss Ward: That's right. Have a great summer, and good luck next year!

[Kids cheer as they rush out of classroom.]

The End

Teacher's Guide

The Riddle Bee

Can you guess the answer?

Using the Play

You already have the perfect set for this play: your own classroom! This makes it easy to perform the play during the last hectic days of school. If you find that the last days are *too* hectic, then take advantage of the language arts aspects of the play and perform this with students at any point during the year.

You may wish to take on the role of Miss Ward in this play. Feel free to change Miss Ward's name to your own, and use the names of actual students in your class as well.

Background

It's difficult for children to contain their excitement at the end of the school year. As happy and excited as children get, however, they are often sad to leave behind the happy memories of the school year. Many teachers choose to leave pets or plants in children's care over the summer months; it serves a practical purpose and provides students with another valuable learning experience.

Book Links

The Riddle Book by Roy McKie (Random House, 1978)

Riddle-Lightful: Oodles of Little Riddle-Poems by J. Patrick Lewis (Knopf, 1998)

Teacher's Pet by Ann M. Martin (Little Apple, 1995)

Touching the Distance: Native American Riddle Poems by Brian Swann (Harcourt Brace, 1998)

Extending the Play

Homophones and Homonyms

In the play, Miss Ward's clever students solve the riddles 1-2-3. In real life, solving riddles can be just as easy—if you know what clues to look for.

Many of the riddles in the play are based on homophones or homonyms. Homophones are words that sound alike but are spelled differently and have different meanings, such as *beat/beet*. Homonyms are words that sound alike and have different meanings, but are spelled the same, such as *beat* (to hit) and *beat* (to win). With students, identify the homophones and homonyms in the play:

carrot/karat

plains/planes

deer/dear

tree leaf/loose-leaf

(piano) key/(answer) key

lean (thin)/lean (slant)

Now that students know the trick, they can make up simple riddles of their own using homophones and homonyms. For example: What can you find on your finger and in your bathtub? A ring! It may help to brainstorm a list of homophones and homonyms with students on the board.

If you wish, gather students' riddles and bind them together to make a class riddle book. Use the book to hold a Riddle Bee in your own classroom.

Pet Care Guide

Do you have any pets or plants in your classroom? Who will take care of them over the summer? Whether it's your job, or something you'll assign to students, your class can play a part in making sure the pet or plant is cared for properly.

As a class, make a Pet Care Guide for your class pet. Your guide should answer the following questions:

What does the pet eat?

How often should the pet be fed and watered?

Where should the pet be kept?

What is the best way to handle the pet?

Does the pet need exercise?

What needs to be done to keep the pet clean?

What should be done if the pet gets sick?

"What Am I?" Riddles

Cut a small slip of paper for each student in your class. On each slip, write the name of a different animal and put the slips in a bag. Ask students to pick one animal name each. Students should write four sentences that describe the animal without using the animal's name. For fun, students can start their sentences in the first person: "I am small. I have eight legs. I spin a web. I eat insects. What am I?" Invite students to read their sentences in front of the class and ask the class to guess what animal the sentences are describing. For a variation, play a "Who Am I?" game using book characters, historical figures, or even the students in your class.

Michael's Cat

by Patrick Daley

Characters

* Storyteller #1
* Storyteller #2
* Neighborhood Chorus
* Michael
* Police Officer
* Baker
* Mail Carrier
* Crossing Guard
* Firefighter
* Pet Store Owner

Props

* a box or cage with a "mouse" inside

A neighborhood street.

Storyteller #1: Michael Minton is having a very bad day.

Storyteller #2: His little cat has run away.

[Michael looks for his cat.]

Michael: Hey, little cat, I'm looking for you.

Storyteller #1: Suddenly Michael heard a very loud meow.

Storyteller #2: Right above him, in a tree, was his little cat.

Michael: Now what will I do?

Chorus: Go ask the police officer. He'll know what to do.

Storyteller #1: So Michael went up to the police officer.

Michael: Mr. Police Officer, I need your help. My little cat is stuck in a tree.

Storyteller #1: The police officer looked up at the tree.

Storyteller #2: He turned to Michael and said:

Police Officer: I can make our town safe from crime.
But a cat in a tree?
I'm stumped this time.

Michael: Now what will I do?

Chorus: Go ask the baker. She'll know what to do.

Storyteller #1: So Michael and the police officer went up to the baker.

Michael: Mrs. Baker, I need your help. My little cat is stuck in a tree.

Storyteller #1: The baker looked up at the tree.

Storyteller #2: She turned to Michael and said:

Baker: I can bake cookies. I can bake cakes.
But a cat in a tree?
I don't have what it takes.

Michael: Now what will I do?

Chorus: Go ask the mail carrier. She'll know what to do.

Storyteller #1: So Michael, the police officer, and the baker went up to the mail carrier.

Michael: Ms. Mail Carrier, I need your help. My little cat is stuck in a tree.

Storyteller 1: The mail carrier looked up at the tree.

Storyteller 2: She turned to Michael and said:

Mail Carrier: I can bring you your mail in rain and snow.
But a cat in a tree?
I just don't know.

Michael: Now what will I do?

Chorus: Go ask the crossing guard. He'll know what to do.

Storyteller #1: So Michael, the policeman, the baker, and the mail carrier went up to the crossing guard.

Michael: Mr. Crossing Guard, I need your help. My little cat is stuck in a tree.

Storyteller #1: The crossing guard looked up at the tree.

Storyteller #2: He turned to Michael and said:

Crossing Guard: I can help you cross the street.
But a cat in a tree?
That has me beat!

Michael: Now what will I do?

Chorus: Go ask the firefighter. She'll know what to do.

Storyteller #1: So Michael, the policeman, the baker, the mail carrier, and the crossing guard went up to the firefighter.

Michael: Ms. Firefighter, I need your help. My little cat is stuck in a tree.

Storyteller #1: The firefighter looked up at the tree.

Storyteller #2: She turned to Michael and said:

Firefighter: I can put out a fire in your house.
But a cat in a tree?
What you need is a mouse!

Michael: A mouse? Where will I find a mouse?

Chorus: Go to the pet store owner. He'll know what to do.

Storyteller #1: So Michael, the policeman, the baker, the mail carrier, the crossing guard, and the firefighter went to the pet store.

Michael: Mr. Pet Store Owner, I need your help. My little cat is stuck in a tree. Ms. Firefighter says we need a mouse.

Storyteller #1: The pet store owner found a mouse in a cage.

Storyteller #2: He turned to Michael and said:

Pet Store Owner: I have frogs that croak and birds that sing.
But for a cat in a tree,
a mouse is just the thing!

Michael: Now what will I do?

Chorus: Go to the tree!

Storyteller #1: So Michael, the police officer, the baker, the mail carrier, the crossing guard, the firefighter, and the pet store owner went to the tree.

Storyteller #2: Michael put the mouse's cage on the ground.

Storyteller #1: The cat saw the mouse. It ran down the tree.

Storyteller #2: Michael picked up his little cat.

Michael: My little cat was in a tree.
I didn't know what to do.
But now my cat is safe and sound.
Thanks to all of you!

The End

Teacher's Guide

Michael's Cat

Using the Play

It's easy to find a role for everyone in your class if you cast the students who don't have major roles in the neighborhood chorus. The chorus can sit or stand in a corner of the staging area, or they can be positioned with the audience to save room.

If you perform this as a skit or full-scale production, consider casting a student in the role of Michael's cat. The cat can crouch on a chair decorated to look like a tree, and jump down when the mouse appears.

Background

There's no doubt that neighborhoods are different all over the country, from crowded city neighborhoods to sprawling suburbs to tight-knit small towns. There is one thing all neighborhoods have in common, however: the people who make them run smoothly.

When you talk about neighborhood helpers, kids will automatically think of police officers and firefighters. It's important to remember that it takes a variety of people to make a neighborhood work: the people who run stores and sell things we need; the people who provide services like repairing appliances and washing clothes; the government workers who keep our streets clean and safe; volunteers who run community programs designed to make life better for everyone; and perhaps most importantly, the neighbors who take care of one another in so many ways.

Book Links

A Busy Day at Mr. Kang's Grocery Store by Alice K. Flanagan (Children's Press, 1997). Look for other neighborhood books from this publisher, too.

Fire Fighters (In My Neighborhood) by Paulette Bourgeois (Kids Can Press, 1998)

Night on Neighborhood Street by Eloise Greenfield (Dial Books, 1991)

Extending the Play

In Your Neighborhood

Before reading the play, tell students that you are going to read a play about neighborhood helpers. Ask students to predict what kinds of characters they may find in such a play. What kinds of people are there to help in their neighborhoods? Write their predictions on the board.

After the play, review your list. Did the play feature any neighborhood helpers they didn't think of? Which neighborhood helpers would they like to see in the play?

As a class, create new rhymes for additional neighborhood characters. Use the format that's used in the play:
(First line tells what the neighborhood helper does.)
But a cat in a tree?
(Last line rhymes with first line.)

This task can be easy if you brainstorm lists of words that rhyme with the last word in the first line after you write that line.

Fun in Store

In the play, Michael and the neighborhood helpers go to a bakery and a pet store. These are just two kinds of stores you may find in a neighborhood. As a class, brainstorm a list of stores in your neighborhood.

After you make the list, ask children to think about what kind of store they would like in their neighborhood that is not on the list. Ask them to imagine that they can open any store they want. What would they sell? Is that something people in your neighborhood would like to buy? When would you be open? How would you let people know about your store?

Have students make posters to announce the "grand opening" of their store. The posters should entice people to shop in the store. Younger students can relay this information through pictures, whereas older students should include text that describes the store.

Practice Possessives

You can use the title of the play, "Michael's Cat," to springboard into possessives practice. Here's one activity that works great at a learning center:

Using index cards, make a name card for every student in your class. Put the cards in one small box. In another small box, create an equal amount of cards with pictures of objects on them (you can use stickers, or cut out pictures from magazines). Good picture words include: *apple, bat, bed, bird, cat, cake, dog, egg, fish, house, key, kite, pig, ring, shoe, tooth,* and *yo-yo.*

At the center, instruct students to pick one card from the name box, and a card from the object box, and then write down the possessive that the two cards form. They should keep going until all the cards have been used.

Great-Grandma's Yo-Yo

by Tonya Leslie

Characters

* Tyler
* Trina
* Great-grandma Annie
* Peddler
* Girl (Annie)
* Boy (Alex)
* City people

Props

* a yo-yo
* a vegetable cart
* a football made of rolled-up newspaper and tape

Act 1

Tyler and Trina are in Great-grandma Annie's living room.

Tyler: I can't believe Mom and Dad left us at Great-grandma Annie's apartment this weekend.

Trina: Yeah! She doesn't have a computer or video games.

Tyler: And her TV is black-and-white!

Trina: How boring! This is going to be one long weekend.

[Great-grandma Annie enters.]

Grandma: It looks like we are going to have a fun long weekend together.

Trina: But Great-grandma, there's nothing to do! We left all our toys at home—even our new yo-yo.

Grandma: When I was your age, we didn't have a lot of toys to play with. In fact, yo-yos only came out when I was ten. Sometimes I played with mine outside with my brother Alex. Other times I cut paper dolls out of magazines. You don't need lots of toys to have fun.

Tyler: Well, what should we do?

Grandma: Here is my old yo-yo. Why don't you go outside and play with it? I always had a fun adventure when I played with my yo-yo. *[She hands the yo-yo to Trina.]*

Tyler: *[Groans and whispers to Trina.]* She had adventures with this old yo-yo? It doesn't glow in the dark, or make noise, or anything.

Trina: *[To Grandma.]* Thanks Great-grandma Annie. Come on Tyler, let's go.

Act 2

A loud noisy street in old New York City. There are pushcarts around selling vegetables, shoes, and tools. The signs on the stores are written in different languages. City people are milling around and talking. Some are sitting on stoops.

Trina: You're right, Tyler. Who wants to play with this dusty old yo-yo? It's made of wood!

Tyler: Yeah, I wish I had my new one. *[He looks around.]* Why is it so noisy out here?

Trina: Everything looks different. I can't read those signs. *[She looks around.]* Hey! Where's Great-grandma's building?

Tyler: That's the building number over there but it looks different. Let's ask that man what's going on.

[They walk over to a peddler.]

Peddler: Tomatoes! Carrots! Get your fresh vegetables here!

Tyler: Excuse me, sir.

Peddler: Yes, son. What do you want? I've got it all. Tomatoes, carrots, onions—anything you need.

Trina: We just want to know what's happening. The streets seem so busy!

Peddler: What's happening? It's a work day! Now, if you're not going to buy anything, don't crowd my cart. I have to make some money, you know. *[Starts yelling.]* Get your fresh vegetables here!

[He walks off.]

Trina: That man was strange. Why is he pushing a cart with vegetables in it? Hey, Tyler, look out!

[A boy and girl are walking down the street. Tyler trips and bumps into a big kid walking down the street. He drops Great-grandma Annie's yo-yo.]

Girl: Hey, watch where you're going!

Tyler: Sorry, I tripped over these crazy rocks in the street.

Girl: *[Laughs.]* Rocks? Those aren't rocks. They're cobblestones, silly.

Boy: You dropped something. *[Picks up the yo-yo.]* Wow! This yo-yo is brand new.

Trina: What are you talking about? That yo-yo is old. I have a newer one that glows!

Boy: What do you mean? No one I know has one. People only talk about buying one, but no one has money.

Tyler: Don't you have any toys?

Boy: Sure we do. I make them myself. *[Holds up football.]* See this? I made it with rolled-up newspaper and tape.

Trina: Not bad. But can you help us? We are looking for building 565.

Boy: I can tell you where that is—for a penny.

Tyler: A penny? What do you want with a penny?

Boy: Are you kidding? You can get lots of stuff for a penny at the candy store on the corner. I could go for an all-day sucker.

Girl: *[To Trina and Tyler.]* Don't listen to him. I'll tell you where 565 is for free. That's my building. It's over there.

Trina: But that building looks different.

Girl: It's looked that way all my life, and I've lived here for a long time.

Trina: I'm really confused. Could we please use your telephone? We should probably call our great-grandmother.

Girl: You could use our telephone if we had one. Hardly anybody on this block does. We all use the phone at the drugstore.

Tyler: Well, I don't know what's going on, but everything seems strange.

Girl: What do you mean?

Trina: People are selling vegetables and shoes and stuff in carts that they push around.

Tyler: Yeah, and the streets are bumpy and not smooth like where we come from.

Trina: Hey! Look, Tyler, there's a horse!

Girl: *[Laughs.]* I bet you don't have horses where you come from either.

Tyler: Not really. People mostly drive cars.

Boy: Cars? I haven't seen that many cars. People around here don't have money for things like that.

Tyler: No cars? *[To Trina.]* I really think something strange is going on here.

Trina: Me, too. *[To girl and boy.]* Why are there so many people outside talking? Don't people around here like to watch television?

Girl: Television? What's that?

Trina: Hmm. No cars. No television. What year is this, anyway?

Girl: What a silly question. It's 1929, of course.

Tyler and Trina: 1929!

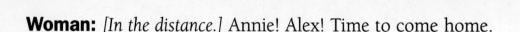

Woman: *[In the distance.]* Annie! Alex! Time to come home.

Boy: Well, we have to go! I hope you find your way home.

Girl: Why don't you go into the building? If you can't find your great-grandmother, just knock on our door. We live in apartment 3B. *[Annie and Alex run off.]*

Trina: Apartment 3B? That's Great-grandma's apartment! Tyler, what's going on?

Tyler: Wait a minute! Great-grandma was ten in 1929. That girl was about ten and she was named Annie just like Great-grandma!

Trina: And she lives in the same apartment. I think that was our Annie—Great-grandma Annie!

Tyler: We took a trip back in time! Now, how will we get back home?

Trina: Let's just try going into the building. *[They start to walk off.]* Hey, Annie took our yo-yo!

Tyler: Well, it's too late now. Let's just try to get home.

Act 3

Back in Great-grandma Annie's apartment . . .

Tyler: *[Opens door.]* Great-grandma? We're back!

Trina: Great-grandma Annie! *[Both kids run to Great-grandma Annie and hug her.]*

Grandma: You must have had fun.

Tyler: We had a real adventure!

Trina: Yes, we met some really cool kids.

Grandma: I knew you could find a way to have fun. And you didn't need any toys at all. Look, you left the yo-yo right on the table. *[She hands it to Trina.]*

Trina: But how. . . ?

Tyler: *[Interrupting.]* Thanks Great-grandma, but I don't think we need that yo-yo anymore. We've had enough adventures for one day. I think I'll stay inside and read a book.

Trina: Me, too!

Grandma: Well, when you are ready for another adventure, just ask for the yo-yo!

The End

Teacher's Guide

Great-Grandma's Yo-Yo

Using the Play

The biggest prop in this play, the vegetable cart, doesn't have to hinder your play performance. If you can't find a real cart or wagon to fill with vegetables (or fake vegetables), have students make a one-dimensional cart out of cardboard for the vendor to "push" down the street.

Students might also enjoy making a backdrop of "old New York City" for the scenes when Tyler and Trina go back in time. Look for photos or illustrations in books to use as reference.

Background

In this play, Tyler and Trina travel back in time to 1929 in New York City.

The Big Apple may be a famous city, but all cities and towns have a rich history worth exploring.

Use the extension activities below to explore what life in your community was like in times past. Whether you "go back in time" ten years or one hundred years, the results will be fascinating.

Book Links

Immigrant Girl: Becky of Eldridge Street by Brett Harvey (Holiday House, 1987)

Irene and the Big, Fine, Nickel by Irene Smalls-Hector (Little, Brown and Co., 1996)

One Room School by Laurence R. Pringle (Boyds Mills Press, 1998)

Extending the Play

Interview an Elder

Tyler and Trina are lucky to have Great-grandma Annie around to tell them about life long ago. Ask students to interview an older person (such as a parent, grandparent, or neighbor) about what life was like when they were a child. Younger students could report the results of the interview by drawing a picture; older students could write up in the interview in a "Q&A" format or in the form of a magazine article.

Encourage students to learn the following information:

What year was it when you were my age?

What was school like?

What kinds of clothes did you wear?

What did you do for fun?

What kinds of food did you eat?

How did you get from place to place?

Where did you shop for food?

How did your town/city look different than it does today?

You may also wish to invite one or more elders to visit your classroom and let the class interview them.

Life Before TV

Great-grandma Annie did not watch television when she was a little girl. So what did she do for fun? Encourage students to brainstorm a list of things to do besides watching television (that includes playing video games and handheld games). Can they think of 50 things to do? How about 100? Ask children to ask their parents and other older people for suggestions. When you've made your classroom list as large as you can, consider turning the ideas into a book to share with other classes. Hold a "No TV" day or week in which students pledge not to watch TV, but try some of the ideas they've come up with instead.

Exploring Your Community

Every community has its own fascinating history. What is the oldest building? How did your town or city get its name? For whom were the streets named? Was anyone famous born there? What important events happened there?

Your class can become "Time Detectives" and explore questions like these. Here are some ways that students of all ages can take a trip back in time:

* Invite a member of the local historical society to come speak to your class. Before the visit, find out what your students are most interested in learning about, and suggest that your speaker focus on these topics. A reporter for your local newspaper may also have some interesting things to say.

* Take a trip to your local library and explore the local history section. You will not be able to take most of these books out of the library, so speak with a librarian beforehand and see if he or she can recommend a particular book or interesting story to share with students. Instead of a picture book at library story time, read a story about your community.

* A trip to the town hall could put you in touch with old photos and displays that show what your town was like long ago. If your town or county has a museum or historical society, pay a visit there, too.

During your explorations, you may gather material from a variety of decades or even centuries. Keep your notes, articles, and photocopies organized in folders separated by date.

Mrs. Toodle Bakes a Pie

by Patrick Daley

Characters

* Storyteller #1
* Storyteller #2
* Mrs. Toodle
* Tommy
* Terry
* Tonya
* Patty
* Paul
* Dan
* Donna

Props

* basket of apples
* TV
* apple pie

Act 1

Mrs. Toodle's house. Tommy, Terry, and Tonya Toodle are watching TV. Mrs. Toodle is in the kitchen.

Storyteller #1: This is a story about a woman and her three children.

Storyteller #2: It all began one beautiful fall day.

Mrs. Toodle: It's a lovely day to bake a pie.

Storyteller #1: Mrs. Toodle went into the living room.

Storyteller #2: Her three children were watching TV.

Mrs. Toodle: Come to the orchard.
Come with me.
We will pick apples
from the apple trees.

Tommy: Oh, no.

Terry: Not me.

Tonya: We would rather watch TV.

Mrs. Toodle: Oh, dear. I see. My children would rather watch TV.

Storyteller #1: So Mrs. Toodle went to her neighbor's house.

Storyteller #2: Patty and Paul came to the door.

Mrs. Toodle: Would you like to come with me?
We'll pick some apples
from the apple trees.

Patty: I will! I will! Yes, indeed!

Paul: I will, too. Don't forget me!

Storyteller #1: So Mrs. Toodle and Patty and Paul went to the orchard.
They picked two big bushels of apples.

Storyteller #2: Later it was time to peel and slice the apples.

Mrs. Toodle: Come here, children.
Come help me.
Let's peel these apples
from the apple tree.

Tommy: Oh, no.

Terry: Not me.

Tonya: We would rather watch TV.

Mrs. Toodle: Oh, dear. I see. My children would rather watch TV.

Storyteller #1: So Mrs. Toodle went to another neighbor's house.

Storyteller #2: Dan and Donna came to the door.

Mrs. Toodle: Would you like to come help me?
We'll peel these apples from the apple tree.

Dan: I will! I will! Yes, indeed!

Donna: I will, too. Don't forget me!

Storyteller #1: So Mrs. Toodle and Dan and Donna peeled all the beautiful red apples.

Storyteller #2: Then it was time to bake the pies.

Storyteller #1: Mrs. Toodle added some cinnamon.

Storyteller #2: And brown sugar, too.

Storyteller #1: Then she put the pies in the oven.

Storyteller #2: Soon the pies were done.

Mrs. Toodle: My pies are done.
Yes, indeed.
I wonder who
will eat them with me?

Tommy: I will! I will!

Terry: Me! Me! Me!

Tonya: Eating pie is better than TV.

Storyteller #1: But Mrs. Toodle shook her head.

Storyteller #2: She looked at her children and this is what she said:

Mrs. Toodle: I'll share my pies
with those who helped me.
Why don't you
just watch TV?

Tommy: Oh, no!

Terry: Dear, me!

Tonya: We missed all the fun. We were watching TV.

Storyteller #1: Mrs. Toodle smiled.

Mrs. Toodle: Don't be sad.
Come with me!
We'll make more pies.
It's fun! You'll see.

Storyteller #1: So Mrs. Toodle and her children picked, peeled, and sliced more apples. They made more apple pies.

Storyteller #2: Then Patty, Paul, Dan, and Donna came over. Everyone ate the delicious pies together.

Mrs. Toodle: Baking pies is so much fun.
I'm glad there's some for everyone!

The End

Teacher's Guide

Mrs. Toodle Bakes a Pie

Using the Play

If you perform this play in your classroom, the door to your room can be the front door of Paul and Patty's house and also of Dan and Donna's house. Instruct the actors to stand outside the door and wait for Mrs. Toodle to knock.

Background

A variation on "The Little Red Hen," this play can be used to kick off a harvesttime theme in your classroom.

No matter where you live in the United States, harvesttime is always an exciting time. The time of year may vary, depending on where you live; there's the early spring vegetable harvest in California or the harvesting of oranges in Florida over the winter. In many parts of the country, however, fall is the traditional harvest season. In times past, harvesttime was cause for a celebration, and a time to enjoy the last fresh crops before the long winter set in. (Thanksgiving, of course, is one modern harvest celebration.)

In the play, Mrs. Toodle is harvesting apples to make a pie. Apples are grown in many parts of the country. Apples are harvested when they are fully ripe, and they are usually picked by hand. The U.S. Apple Association estimates that the average American eats 46 pounds of apples in a year, including processed apple products such as apple juice and applesauce. That's a lot of apples!

Book Links

Apple Picking Time by Michelle Benoit Slawson (Dragonfly, 1998)

Fall Harvest by Gail Saunders-Smith (Capstone Press, 1998)

The Little Red Hen by Harriet Ziefert (Puffin, 1995)

Picking Apples & Pumpkins by Amy and Richard Hutchings (Cartwheel Books, 1994)

Extending the Play

Story Sequence

After reading the play, discuss the process that Mrs. Toodle went through. Ask: *What did Mrs. Toodle do first to make the pie?* (She asked Paul and Patty to help her pick the apples.) *What did she do after she picked the apples?* (She asked Dan and Donna to help her peel the apples.) *What did she do next?* (She baked the apple pie.)

You may also wish to discuss the characters. Ask: *Why do you think Mrs. Toodle's children didn't help her?* (They were lazy; they thought watching TV was more fun than picking apples.) *What do you think they will do the next time their mother asks for their help?* (Answers may vary.)

The Little Red Hen

As a class, read *The Little Red Hen* by Harriet Ziefert, or another version of the tale. Discuss similarities between this classic tale and the play. Make a simple chart that illustrates those similarities.

Work together to write a play based on *The Little Red Hen,* and perform your play along with "Mrs. Toodle Bakes a Pie" for a double feature.

Apple Fun

If possible, arrange an apple-picking trip to a local apple orchard or to a farmer's market to look at all the different varieties of apples available.

If you are able to take home several different kinds of apples, cut the apples into pieces and allow students to taste each kind. For each apple they taste, ask students to write a description: What color was it? Was it hard or soft? Was it juicy? Was it sweet or tart? When they've tasted all the apples, take a poll to see which apples students liked best. Then graph your results.

If you are allowed access to your school's cafeteria or a cooking area, students can follow directions and practice measuring skills to make this simple apple crisp recipe (the next best thing to Mrs. Toodle's apple pie!):

Apple Crisp
6 medium apples
1 tablespoon lemon juice
1 tablespoon water
3/4 cup firmly-packed brown sugar
1 cup baking mix
1 teaspoon cinnamon
1/2 cup margarine

1. Have an adult heat the oven to 375°.
2. Peel the apples. Core the apples. Then slice the apples.
3. Place the apples in an 8" square pan.
4. Sprinkle the lemon juice and water on the apples.
5. In a bowl, combine the brown sugar, baking mix, cinnamon, and margarine until crumbly.
6. Sprinkle the crumbly mix over the apples.
7. Have an adult put the pan in the oven. Bake for 40 to 45 minutes or until the apples are tender. Let cool before you eat.

I Take My Senses Everywhere

by Betsy Franco

Props

* book
* leaves
* cookie
* sand in a container
* candy or apple
* kitten's tail made of yarn or felt

Hearing 1 & 2: I hear. *[Cup ears.]*

Sight 1 & 2: I see. *[Use fingers to make circles around eyes.]*

Smell 1 & 2: I smell. *[Touch noses.]*

Taste 1 & 2: I taste. *[Open mouths and point to them.]*

Touch 1 & 2: I like to touch things, too. *[Show 10 fingers.]*

All: I take my senses everywhere *[Spread arms out.]*

and so do all of you. *[Point to audience.]*

Child 1: I use them when I climb a tree,

[Pretends to climb a tree.]

and when I hear a frog.

[The frog croaks and leaps.]

Child 2: I use them when I brush my teeth, *[Pretends to brush teeth.]*

and when I pat a dog. *[Pats dog.]*

Hearing 1: I hear the early morning train. Clang, clang.

I hear a quacking duck. Quack, quack.

Hearing 2: I hear the sound of falling rain. *[Claps softly.]*

I hear the ice cream truck! Jing-a-ling.

Sight 1:   I use my eyes to watch the stars. *[Pretends to use a telescope.]*

I watch the leaves in fall. *[Throws up leaves.]*

Sight 2:   I use my eyes to read a book. *[Reads a book.]*

I watch a home-run ball! *[Pretends to bat a ball.]*

Smell 1:   I use my nose to smell a rose. *[Pretends to smell a rose.]*

I smell my stinky shoes. *[Smells shoe and wrinkles nose.]*

Smell 2:   I use my nose to smell a skunk *[Skunk walks by, child backs off.]*

and fresh-baked cookies, too! *[Smells a cookie.]*

Taste 1:   My mouth can taste a lemon. *[Puckers up lips.]*

My mouth can taste the sea. *[Sticks out tongue.]*

Taste 2:   My mouth can taste a popsicle. *[Pretends to lick a popsicle.]*

My favorite taste is sweet! *[Holds up candy.]*

Touch 1:   I touch the sand that's on the beach.

[Picks up sand in a container]

I touch a kitten's tail. _[Touches the kitten's tail.]_

Touch 2:   I touch your hand to do "high five."

[Does high five with Touch 1.]

I touch a slimy snail! _[Touches snail.]_

Hearing 1 & 2: I use my ears. _[Cup ears.]_

Sight 1 & 2:   My eyes. _[Use fingers to make circles around eyes.]_

Smell 1 & 2:   My nose. _[Touch nose.]_

Taste 1 & 2:   My mouth. _[Open mouths and point to them.]_

Touch 1 & 2:   My fingers, too. _[Show 10 fingers.]_

All: I take my senses everywhere. _[Spread arms out.]_

and so do all of you! _[Point to audience.]_

The End

Teacher's Guide

I Take My Senses Everywhere

Using the Play

With its rhyming lines and simple text, this play is a good choice for younger readers. Students will enjoy taking on the roles of the five senses: hearing, sight, smell, taste, and touch. When assigning roles, note that the animal roles are non-speaking parts.

This play also stands by itself as a poem. You may wish to copy the poem, without the stage directions, onto chart paper and read the lines together as a class before performing the play.

Background

We humans use our senses to tell us about the world around us. Our five senses are:

Hearing: Sounds are vibrations. When sound vibrations reach the ear, they travel inside the ear canal to the eardrum. As the eardrum vibrates, nerves send messages to the brain, which interprets the sound.

Sight: We see objects because light reflects off them. The light enters the eye through the pupil, and images are projected onto cells called rods and cones. The rods and cones then send the images to the brain.

Smell: When a smell enters a nose, it is trapped by tiny hairs. Then nerves send the messages about smells to the brain.

Taste: Thousands of tiny taste buds on the tongue detect the different tastes of the things we eat and drink.

Touch: Just under the skin are nerves that send messages to the brain about the way things feel. Nerves are more concentrated in areas such as fingertips, making them more sensitive.

Book Links

City Sounds by Craig Brown (Greenwillow Books, 1992)

My Five Senses by Aliki (HarperCollins, 1989)

Night Sounds, Morning Colors by Rosemary Wells (Dial Books, 1994)

Riddles About the Senses by Jacqueline A. Ball (Silver Burdett Press, 1989)

Extending the Play

How Many Senses?

This quick game is a great introduction to a senses unit. Begin by writing the name of an activity on the board. Then ask students to count how many senses they use when performing this activity. For example:

* lining up when the bell rings (hearing and sight)
* playing baseball (hearing, sight, touch)
* eating lunch (touch, taste, smell, sight)
* listening to the radio (hearing)

Time for Rhyme

Point out that the lines in the play rhyme. How can we tell that the words rhyme? We use our sense of hearing.

Write out the pairs of words from the play that rhyme: *frog/dog, duck/truck, fall/ball,* and *tail/snail.* Then lead the class in a Rhyming Bee. First, write the words on the list below in a column on the chalkboard (or come up with some words of your own). Divide the class into two teams. Have each team take turns coming up with a rhyme for one of the words. (Students who are able can write their words on the chalkboard.) The whole class wins when there's a rhyme for each of the words on your list.

Word List

say	see	eye	row
blue	bat	feet	boat
sing	face	lean	rice
sun	rain	cold	four
ate	sand		

Sense Centers

Turn your classroom into a "Museum of the Senses." Designate a small desk, table, or shelf for each of the five senses. Spend one day each week creating something that can be experienced with each sense or that demonstrates each sense. Then display your creations at the sense centers. For example:

Hearing: Make music makers with lidded containers filled with dried beans.

Sight: Paint colorful pictures.

Smell: Instruct half the class to draw pictures of things they like to smell (flowers, the ocean); instruct the other half to draw pictures of things they don't like to smell (a skunk, pollution).

Taste: Make a simple recipe, such as trail mix or no-bake cookies, that can be shared at the center. Or make a graph of the class's favorite foods.

Touch: Use materials such as felt, feathers, cotton balls, rocks, and sand to make touch-and-feel collages.

The Garden Meal

by Patrick Daley and Amy Laura Dombro

Characters

* Storyteller #1
* Storyteller #2
* Mary
* Mora
* Paul
* Mom

Props

* a pail
* a bowl
* pictures or paintings of lettuce, tomatoes, carrots, radishes, watermelon, strawberries

Act 1

Storyteller #1: It was dinnertime.

Storyteller #2: Mary, Mora, and Paul came into the kitchen.

Mary: Mom! Mom!

Mora: We're home.

Paul: And we are REALLY hungry!

Mom: I am glad you are home. I am glad you are hungry. Tonight we are having a special meal.

Mary: I bet we are having hot dogs.

Mora: I bet we are having hamburgers.

Paul: We are having pizza! I know we are having pizza!

Mom: No. We are not having hot dogs or hamburgers. We are not having pizza, either. Your dinner is out in the garden.

Paul: Dinner from the garden? I'm not sure about this.

Act 2

Storyteller #1: Mother got a great big pail.

Storyteller #2: They all went out to the garden.

Mom: First we will pick some lettuce.

Mary: This lettuce is nice and green.

Mora: Gross. This piece has a bug on it.

Paul: Lettuce for dinner? I'm not sure about this.

Mom: Now we need some tomatoes.

Mary: Here is a big red tomato.

Mora: This one is green. We don't want that.

Paul: Tomatoes for dinner? I'm not sure about this.

Mother: Now we need some vegetables from the ground.

Mary: I found some carrots.

Mora: I found some radishes.

Paul: Carrots and radishes for dinner? I'm not sure about this.

Storyteller #1: They filled the pail with the lettuce, the tomatoes, the carrots, and the radishes.

Storyteller #2: Then they took the vegetables into the kitchen.

Act 3

Storyteller #1: Inside, they washed the lettuce, the tomatoes, the carrots, and the radishes.

Storyteller #2: Then they chopped the lettuce, the tomatoes, the carrots, and the radishes.

Storyteller #1: Then Mom put the lettuce, the tomatoes, the carrots, and the radishes in a great big bowl.

Mom: Here is some fresh bread to go with your garden meal.

Mary: This is a salad.

Mora: And it is delicious!

Paul: Hey! This is pretty good.

Storyteller #2: Soon they were finished eating the garden meal.

Mary: The dishes are clean.

Mora: It's time for dessert.

Paul: What will we have?

Mom: Let's go back to the garden and you will see.

Storyteller #1: They went back out into the garden.

Mary: I see watermelon. That's what I want.

Mora: I see berries. That's what I want.

Paul: I see watermelon and berries. I want both.

Storyteller #2: The children went back into the house.

Storyteller #1: They had watermelon and berries for dessert.

Mom: I think the garden is a good place for a meal. What do you think?

Mary: Yes! This meal was delicious.

Mora: Yes! I am very full!

Paul: The garden is a great place for a meal. I am sure about this!

The End

Teacher's Guide

The Garden Meal

eat comes from. A garden is a wonderful place to introduce students to all kinds of concepts, from how plants grow, to eating healthy foods.

A small number of schools in the country have started school gardens. Students tend to the vegetables grown there, harvest the vegetables, and then eat the food when it is prepared for them in the school cafeteria. It may be hard to believe, but children will try and enjoy a variety of "yucky" foods when they have a hand in growing and preparing it—just like Paul in the play.

Using the Play

To create a "garden" in your classroom, have students make small signs with pictures of lettuce, tomatoes, carrots, radishes, watermelon, strawberries, and other fruits and vegetables. Attach the signs to popsicle sticks, and plant the sticks in small flowerpots. Arrange the pots around your set to give the effect of garden rows.

Book Links

City Green by Dyanne Disalvo-Ryan (William Morrow and Co., 1994)

Miss Emma's Wild Garden by Anna Grassnickle Hines (Greenwillow, March 1997)

Mr. Carey's Garden by Jane Cutler (Houghton Mifflin Company, 1996)

Background

With processed food so much a part of our diets, it's easy to forget where the food we

Extending the Play

Eat Your Veggies

After reading the play, discuss the characters' responses to the garden meal. Ask: *At first, how did Paul feel about eating garden vegetables for supper?* (He didn't think he would like it.) *How did Paul feel by the end of the meal?* (He liked it.)

Ask students to discuss how they feel about vegetables. Do students like them or dislike them? Brainstorm a list of vegetables that students like to eat. Ask students to name their favorite vegetable (even kids who only like french fries can name potatoes) and graph the results.

Explain that the government recommends that people eat five servings of vegetables and three servings of fruit daily. Ask students to keep track of what they eat in one day, either by making a list or drawing a picture after each meal. The next day, review the lists as a class. How many vegetables and fruits did each student eat? Figure out the class average. Do you need to improve that number? Discuss ways students could include more vegetables and fruits in their diet.

Your Own Garden Meal

Making a garden meal is something you can do in your classroom. If you have access to a cafeteria, wash, peel, and slice (with adult help or supervision) any number of fresh vegetables, such as lettuce, tomatoes, cucumber, celery, carrots, spinach, radishes, or mushrooms. If you don't have access to a kitchen, wash and prepare the ingredients at home and let students combine them in the classroom. Combine the ingredients in a large bowl, toss, and you've got a garden meal! If possible, provide a variety of salad dressings for students to choose from.

When you're done with your salad, ask students to write out the recipe for your garden meal.

Ideally, a local gardener will allow you to visit their garden and pick your own veggies for your garden meal, or at least let your students see where veggies come from.

Start With a Seed

Students can find out how seeds grow, right in the classroom. Provide each student with a small cup (an eggshell half works well, too), a small amount of potting soil, a few vegetable seeds (a bean seed or radish seed will sprout fairly easily), and a sheet of plastic wrap. Have students plant the seeds just under the dirt and water the seeds. Students should cover their cup loosely with plastic wrap to retain moisture, then label the containers with the name of the seed and the date. While students are planting, explain that seeds need four things to sprout: moisture, warmth, air, and light. Discuss ways to provide the seeds with what they need. Keep them in a warm, well-lit place; water them regularly; and make sure the plastic wrap isn't too tight so that the seeds get enough air. Students can keep records of when they water seeds, when seeds sprout, and how the seedlings grow.

A Surprise for the Tooth Fairy

by Sheila Sweeny

Characters

* Girl #1
* Dad
* Tooth Fairy
* Tooth Fairy's boss
* Boy #1
* Mom #1
* Girl #2
* Mom #2
* Kid chorus

Props

* blankets and pillow to make a child's bed
* a small stone (to represent a tooth)
* a quarter
* a magic wand
* paper and crayons

Act 1

Inside Girl #1's bedroom.

Girl #1: Jiggle, jiggle, jiggle.
My tooth is starting to wiggle.
Wiggle, wiggle, wow!
My tooth is out now!
[Holds out pretend tooth for audience to see.]

Dad: Put your tooth under your pillow. Then maybe the tooth fairy will leave you a surprise. *[Dad leaves.]*

Girl #1: *[Puts tooth under pillow and falls asleep.]* Goodnight, tooth. I hope I don't see you in the morning!

Tooth Fairy: *[Walks in, checks under the pillow, then examines the tooth.]* What a shiny tooth! I love shiny teeth! This girl did a good job brushing her teeth!

[The Tooth Fairy leaves a shiny coin under the girl's pillow. She taps the pillow with her wand and then leaves.]

Girl #1: *[Wakes up.]*
Jiggle, jiggle, jiggle.
My tooth was starting to wiggle.
Wiggle, wiggle, wow!
I have a quarter now!

Act 2

Inside the tooth fairy's castle.

Tooth Fairy: Another shiny tooth for my collection. Oh, I love teeth.
Every bright, shiny one of them. *[The tooth fairy begins tapping her own teeth.
Then she begins to look worried.]* Wait! What's this?

> Jiggle, jiggle, jiggle.
> *My tooth is starting to wiggle.*
> Wiggle, wiggle, wow!
> *My tooth is out now!*
> *[Holds out pretend tooth for audience to see.]*

Tooth Fairy's boss: That's a pretty tooth to add to your collection.

Tooth Fairy: But who will leave a surprise for me?

Tooth Fairy's boss: Tooth fairies don't get surprises. They give them!

Tooth Fairy: Not even a teeny, weeny surprise?

Tooth Fairy's boss: Not even a teeny weeny surprise. And you should get
back to work. There were a lot of loose teeth today.

[The tooth fairy leaves, looking a little sad.]

Act 3

Inside Boy #1's bedroom.

Boy #1: Jiggle, jiggle, jiggle.
My tooth is starting to wiggle.
Wiggle, wiggle, wow!
My tooth is out now!
[Holds out pretend tooth for audience to see.]

Mom #1: Put your tooth under your pillow. Then maybe the tooth fairy will leave you a surprise. *[Mom leaves scene.]*

Boy #1: *[Puts tooth under pillow and pretends to fall asleep, but really is still awake.]* Goodnight, tooth. I hope I don't see you in the morning!

Tooth Fairy: *[Walks in, checks under the pillow, then examines the tooth, but she looks very sad and is not too excited to see a new tooth.]* Oh, boy. A shiny tooth. This is one lucky boy. He gets a big surprise. I wish someone would give me a surprise for the tooth I lost today.

[The tooth fairy leaves a shiny coin under the boy's pillow. She sadly taps the pillow with her wand, sighs, and then leaves. The boy peeks out from under the covers to watch her leaving. He has heard everything.]

Boy #1: The tooth fairy looked so sad. But I know how to make her smile again!

Act 4

In school.

Girl #2: Jiggle, jiggle, jiggle.
My tooth is starting to wiggle.
Wiggle, wiggle, wow!
My tooth is out now!
[Holds out pretend tooth for audience to see.]

Boy #1: Are you going to put your tooth under your pillow, so the tooth fairy will leave you a surprise?

Girl #2: Yes!

Boy #1: Would you like to surprise the tooth fairy?

Girl #2: Yes!

Boy #1: Well, last night I saw the tooth fairy. She was sad because she had lost her tooth. And nobody was going to leave her a surprise.

Kid chorus: Let's surprise her!

[Kids begin getting out paper and crayons.]

Boy #1: Let's draw her a picture.

Kid chorus: *[To Girl #2.]* And you can leave it under your pillow tonight.

Girl #2: We can write "Thank you" on the picture.

Kid chorus: And the picture should have lots of shiny teeth!

Boy #1: Let's get started!

[Kids all work together to make a big, beautiful picture for the tooth fairy.]

Act 5

Inside Girl #2's bedroom.

Mom #2: Put your tooth under your pillow. Then maybe the tooth fairy will leave you a surprise. *[Mom leaves.]*

Girl #2: *[Whispers.]* Or maybe I will leave *her* a surprise. *[Giggles as she puts tooth and picture under pillow.]*

Tooth Fairy: *[Walks in, checks under the pillow, looks a little surprised.]* A shiny tooth! And a . . . a . . . a picture for me! I love shiny teeth! I love pictures for me! I love surprises!

[The tooth fairy does a little happy dance around the room. The girl peeks out from under the covers and smiles.]

Tooth Fairy: *[Dancing.]*

      Jiggle, jiggle, jiggle.

      My tooth was starting to wiggle.

      Wiggle, wiggle, wow!

      I have a surprise, now!

The End

Teacher's Guide

A Surprise for the Tooth Fairy

frightening to children, the friendly tooth fairy can help children learn how to care for their teeth. A popular figure in folklore, the tooth fairy is an international phenomenon loved by children and parents everywhere.

Book Links

Andrew's Loose Tooth by Robert N. Munsch (Cartwheel Books, 1998)

Dear Tooth Fairy: The True Story of How the Tooth Fairy Came to Be by Kath Mellentin (Little Simon, 1997)

The Story of the Tooth Fairy by Tom Paxton (William Morrow and Co., 1996)

Food for Healthy Teeth by Helen Frost (Capstone Press, 1998)

Using the Play

To set the stage for this play, consider dividing your stage area into three sections: the Tooth Fairy's castle on stage left, a bedroom that can be used for each of the children on center stage, and a school setting (such as a table and chairs) on stage right.

Your set designers will have fun imagining what the Tooth Fairy's castle looks like. You may want to encourage them to decorate the castle as creatively as possible.

Extending the Play

Tooth Tales

Losing a first tooth is an important occasion in most children's lives. Many adults can still recall the experience with great detail. Your students can make sure they never forget this momentous day.

Ask students who have already lost

Background

February is National Children's Dental Health Month. While the subject of tooth care can be unappealing and even

teeth to write about the experience in an essay titled, "The Time I Lost My First Tooth." Prompt them with questions to help them recall detail:

Where were you?

What were you doing when it happened?

Were you surprised when it happened?

Did somebody help you pull out the tooth?

Did it hurt?

Did you leave your tooth under your pillow that night?

What did the tooth fairy bring you?

Have students share their stories with the class and discuss the similarities and differences between their experiences.

If your students are younger and just beginning to lose teeth, give the assignment to each student as his or her first tooth is lost. Keep a running list of students who have lost a tooth. If possible, use an instant camera to photograph each child's new, toothless smile and use the photos to decorate a dental health bulletin board or center.

Thank You, Tooth Fairy

In the play, the boys and girls make a picture to thank the tooth fairy. Students can make their own thank-you cards to keep on hand to leave for the tooth fairy the next time they lose a tooth.

To make the cards, instruct students to fold an 8 ½" x 11" piece of paper in half. On the front of the cards, students can draw a picture of the tooth fairy. Ask students to imagine what she might look like. On the inside, encourage students to

write a note of thanks and perhaps tell something about themselves, too.

Tooth Tips

Students can make colorful tooth care posters to encourage good dental habits. First review these dental health tips with students:

Brush your teeth at least twice a day.

Use dental floss.

Visit the dentist for regular checkups.

Eat healthy foods like vegetables.

Eat foods high in calcium, like milk and green vegetables.

Avoid sugary snacks.

Have students create a poster that encourages people to follow one of these tips. Ask students to think about the best way to get their message across. Display the posters during National Children's Dental Health Month in February.

Notes

Notes

Notes